Progressing from

Life

Through

Death

and Beyond

Incredible Stories of People
Who Have Died & Lived To Tell About It

DR. J. ROLAND GIARDETTI

WESTBOW
PRESS°
A DIVISION OF THOMAS NELSON
& ZONDERVAN

WestBow Press books may be ordered through booksellers or by contacting:

WestBow Press
A Division of Thomas Nelson & Zondervan
1663 Liberty Drive
Bloomington, IN 47403
www.westbowpress.com
844-714-3454

I have tried to recreate events, locales and conversations from my memories of them. To maintain their anonymity in some instances I have changed the names of individuals and places, I may have also changed some identifying characteristics and details such as physical properties, occupations and places of residence.

Scripture quotations are taken from the Revised Standard Version of the Bible, copyright © 1946, 1952, and 1971 the Division of Christian Education of the National Council of the Churches of Christ in the United States of America. Used by permission. All rights reserved.

ISBN: 979-8-3850-1089-9 (sc)
ISBN: 979-8-3850-1090-5 (e)

Library of Congress Control Number: 2023920572

Print information available on the last page.

WestBow Press rev. date: 12/06/2023

CONTENTS

PART 1

PART 2

PART 3

PART 4

DEDICATION

For all our dear family, including seven adult children,
their spouses, and our twenty-three grandchildren,
in Canada and the United States.

The briefest possible compression of Saint Paul's letter to the Hebrews about the meaning of faith is:

"Faith is being sure of what you hope for."

This book is about a lot of hope and faith. It has taken twenty-five years to reproduce these miraculous stories and it is the hope of the author that all those who venture here are prepared to meet the Author and Healer of all life.

...Jesus said to him, "I will come and heal him." But the centurion answered him. "Lord, I am not worthy to have you come under my roof, but only say the word and my servant will be healed. For I am a man under authority, with soldiers under me; and I say to one, 'Go,' and he goes, and to another 'Come,' and he comes, and to my slave, 'Do this,' and he does it. When Jesus heard him, he marveled, and said to those who followed him, "Truly I say to you, not even in Israel have I found such faith.... And to the centurion Jesus said, "Go; be it done for you as you have believed." And the servant was healed at that very moment. (Mt 8.7-13)

ACKNOWLEDGMENTS

The author is indebted to many sources of assistance. First is my dear wife Erin, not only for her steadfast love and kindness over fifty-six years, but her great amount of help in the writing of this book. All the members of our family are also thanked for their prayer support over a lifetime of trials. Special thanks are given to our dear friend in Christ, David S., for his good counsel and support over many years. We are very grateful for Gayle M. and Anita and Edwin A. and many others who have faithfully blessed us with their fervent prayers. Editing was of great help by Judy M., Denny and Margaret Ann W. *Without counsel plans go wrong, but with many advisers they succeed.* (Prov 15.22). Thanks, are also given to many staff members at WestBow Press for their helpful guidance in the publication of *Progressing from Life Through Death and Beyond.*

And before all,

Thanks be to God!

THE MEANINGS OF DEATH
AND SURVIVAL

The second half of this book is all about people of Christian faith who have actually or almost died with all the medical indicators. While there may or may not have been signed and dated medical certificates of death, these stories are, nonetheless, about people who were dead or nearly dead and came to life again or survived near death. The mystery of how this happens in each case is attributed to faith and calling upon the mercy of God in the name of Jesus Christ.

"Then Mary…fell at his (Jesus) feet saying to him, 'Lord if you had been here my brother (Lazarus) would not have died.'" (John 11:32)

The following testimonies are presented as reasons for hope and not as spectacular dramatizations of individual experiences. To testify in the legal definition is to provide verbal affirmation that the witness saw and/or heard specific events as he/she reports under oath to tell the truth. Under these circumstances it would be unusual for someone to falsify the details of their actual or near-death experience.

It is also imperative that a clear distinction be made between death followed by survival and death followed by an afterlife experience. ADE represents After Death Experience, and NDE designates Near Death Experience. The ADE stories have become the subject of recent movies with bright lights at the end of tunnels, sweet smells, beautiful fields of flowers and warm feelings of comfort and peace. Both the ADE and the NDE have been recorded in personal testimonies throughout history.

More recently NDE may have resulted when a medical intervention was applied to prevent death, as is common in cardiac surgery or the many techniques for preventing death from trauma or stroke.

The stories in part 2 are reported as well as can be stated and are true and clear accounts of the persons and actual events. Most of the names and places of their stories have been changed upon request to protect their privacy and their desire to remain without notoriety.

Following the publication of Dead Man Watching in 2017 by WestBow Press, the author became aware by several providential meetings that his story was not so unique and not the "lone ranger" he thought he was.

In the New Testament there are four people named who were dead for various amounts of time and were then called back to life. Lazarus is the most well-known and dramatic case, as his grieving sister, Martha, complained to Jesus that his body would surely be corrupted and create a stench after four days in the tomb. The other three cases did not include a body that was long dead. They are the stories of Tabitha (Matt. 27:50-54), Eutychus (Acts 9:36-42), the widow's son (Luke 7:11-17) and the daughter of Jairus (Mark 5:21-43). These were all cases which brought attention to the life and earthly ministry of Jesus Christ, son of Mary and His earthly father Joseph of Nazareth.

In the personal case of the author, over twenty-five years ago, the audible voice was my dear wife Erin, praying in tongues (glossolalia) over my recently announced corpse. Looking back on that whole episode, the impact on the medical staff on the scene was observed to have been somewhere between shock and amazement, as Erin prayed. over the patient the staff had just watched die. They had no idea who she was or how a stranger dressed in scrubs got into the emergency room without a proper staff ID tag. This impact was like some of the reactions to the rising of the dead in the New Testament accounts. What is going on here? How is this all happening?

Going back to the issue of my own story of survival, which is not as rare as I originally thought, I remain eager to use the experience as a one-on-one evangelism tool. The standard ice breaker is "you see and are talking to a dead man." This is not a common conversation starter. It is usually effective, and my audience frequently wants to know more.

The first question is usually "how long were you dead?" With a smile my answer is that "dead people don't know what time it is, because time has stopped." That line is always followed by "I sure am glad my next stop was not the morgue."

This leads to one of my first encounters with another survivor of death story. Sitting next to a middle-aged woman on an airplane ride to our winter home in Florida, after my standard icebreaker the lady told me about her mother's death and her being carted off to the morgue, the only room in a hospital I have never been to.

The next experience is the one that pushed me over the edge to write part 2 of the book. After my typical opener, this elderly man listened patiently and asked no questions, which was not the usual response. Instead, he almost bragged that he had died on "three" separate occasions! Now I got to be the one shocked, and you will find his amazing story in the second part of the book: The Death and Survival of Hans x 3.

This book is presented to the reader under the two main categories already described: ADE and NDE. The author moves forward through these dramatic stories of death-defying survivals, while there remains the prototype following account of the afterlife of the rich man and Lazarus in the New Testament.

INTRODUCTORY TEXT ON DEATH

The Parable of the Rich Man and Lazarus

"Will they be persuaded if someone should rise from the dead?"

(Luke 16: 19-31)

"There was a rich man who dressed in purple garments and fine linen and dined sumptuously each day. And lying at his door was a poor man named Lazarus covered with sores, who would gladly have eaten his fill of the scraps that fell from the rich man's table. Dogs even used to come and lick his sores. When the poor man died, he was carried away by angels to the bosom of Abraham. The rich man also died and was buried, and from the netherworld, where he was in torment, he raised his eyes and saw Abraham far off and Lazarus at his side. And he cried out, 'Father Abraham, have pity on me. Send Lazarus to dip the tip of his finger in water and cool my tongue, for I am suffering torment in these flames.' Abraham replied, 'My child, remember that you received what was good during your lifetime while Lazarus likewise received what was bad, but now he is comforted here, whereas you are tormented. Moreover, between us and you a great chasm is established to prevent anyone from crossing who might wish to go from our side to yours or from your side to ours.' He said, 'Then I beg you, Father, send him to my father's house for I have five brothers, so that he may warn them lest they too come to this place of torment.' But Abraham replied, 'They have Moses and the prophets. Let them listen to them.' He said, 'Oh no,

Father Abraham, but if someone from the dead goes to them, they will repent.' Then Abraham said, 'If they will not listen to Moses and the prophets, will they be persuaded if someone should rise from the dead?"

This book is presented to the reader with respect for the Biblical accounts of the effect of death regarding its finality. The message is profoundly clear that "even if someone should rise from the dead" one may choose not to believe. It is the sincere hope and prayer of the author that these stories of death and near death might be of value in considering the meaning and realities of Faith leading to Life after death.

INTRODUCTION

The Beginning of the End

by Erin
The wife's testimony about her husband's life

J. Roland Giardetti was born in the mid 1940's. He was raised as a Catholic, and eventually we met and were married in the Catholic Church. However, after many years of Catholic schools and untested faith, he needed to be confronted with the clear presentation of the Gospel of Jesus Christ and accept it.

After a few years of marriage, we became aware of a new movement in the Catholic Church called the *Charismatic Renewal*. One Sunday evening we found our way to a special talk by a well-known French-Canadian priest from Quebec. Our attendance was to be quite pivotal. The preceding experience was our preparation for what was beyond.

Sometime earlier we had gone on vacation to New York City and ended up in Greenwich Village at a Sunday flea market in a Jewish neighborhood. In the middle of a huge crowd Roland's attention was riveted to a red-headed girl in a brilliant white shirt, standing slightly above the crowd. She was shouting phrases from the Bible as loudly as she could. Roland could just make out *For God so loved the world that He sent His only Son, that whoever believes in Him should not perish, but have eternal life.* (John 3.16) Suddenly an overripe tomato hit her with great velocity and created the image that she had been shot. Many more tomatoes followed, until she was blown off her soap box in a shower of red. It was a real shock. The whole scene looked like an actual murder. The many familiar stories of saints and martyrs had previously made little impression on Roland. Here she was…suffering for her faith! He was brought to tears and could do nothing to help or reverse this very real-looking martyrdom. An epiphany had happened and for the first time in his adult life he was awakened to the suffering of Christ and the shed blood of the martyrs.

The timing was providential for us. Upon returning to our home that summer we went to listen for the first and only time to the priest from Quebec. His two-hour sermon was the best we had ever heard, and as trained and practicing high school teachers we were amazed that he held the capacity audience on the edge of their seats for the entire time. The conclusion included a call to come forward. We saw many of the crowd moving to the basement stairs in the front of the St. Agnes RC church for coffee and donuts…so we thought. However, to our amazement when we arrived, he was praying over each one, some of whom fell to the floor without injury. He was doing what is done for *Confirmation, Holy Orders and prayer for the sick (Extreme Unction)*, which includes the laying on of hands.

Often in His ministry, Jesus healed the sick by reaching out and touching those who needed healing. Once He healed a woman who secretly touched the hem of his garment, hoping to be healed. *Jesus said. "Someone touched me; for I perceive that power has gone forth from me… And he said to her, "Daughter, your faith has made you well; go in peace."* (Lk 8.46,48)

Following this second pivotal event, we started attending the *Life in the Spirit Seminars*. These meetings were held in small group settings. The lessons were basic evangelism, emphasizing the role and power of the Holy Spirit in a believer's life. The impact was substantial. Roland's logical mind was working overtime against some of the message with the age-old criticism of Christianity. *If God is so good and merciful, why is there so much evil and suffering in the world?*

We had many heated discussions on the topic. He was ready to quit the sessions, but one night at the prayer meetings that we also attended, another pivotal event took place. An announcement was made about a men's *Cursillo* (a short course in Christ) to take place the following weekend, an eight-hour trip away. I spoke to one of the leaders and asked him to reach out to Roland with a personal invitation. Within minutes he was surrounded by a small group of the team. They gave him some details and insisted that he could and should call into work for a personal day to attend the *Cursillo*.

The logistics of travelling hundreds of miles for a weekend retreat were impossible. But the next morning at 4:00 a.m., he was in a van bound for the monastery in Winnipeg, Manitoba, as one of twelve men, singing songs of praise.

The tightly packed course was a series of inspiring lectures and discussion groups leading to an opportunity for personal conversion. All was going very well until he found himself in need of some quiet time to process everything that was going on in his mind and spirit. He found the beautiful chapel of the monastery and thought he was all alone, privately praying in the front. After a long period of silence and questioning God, he snapped, called out to Jesus to forgive him for his sin, and began weeping uncontrollably for some time. When he finally was able to get up, he turned around he discovered a little nun in the last pew. She had quietly been there for the entire emotional breakdown. She simply smiled and blessed him as he left the chapel. Just as the red-headed evangelist in New York remains an unidentified person with significant impact on his life, so the little nun in the chapel is a blessed memory to this day.

He returned a changed man from the *Cursillo*. He had experienced a Pauline conversion, knocked off his intellectual horse and would never be the same. I was amazed when he returned home and could see the great change. He was full of joy…happy and loving (refer to the *fruits of the spirit* in Galatians 5:22-23). The following Monday he went back to high school teaching, wearing the substantial crucifix he was given at the conclusion of the *Cursillo*. It must have looked to faculty members and students like he had just become a deacon or some form of Christian minister.

Life went on with our four daughters and one son. We were blessed with a tranquil and sometimes challenging life on a hobby farm 25 miles out of town. It was the Great White North, halfway between East and West. His little joke was that he traveled from Eastern to Western Canada every day of the school year because the geographic center of the transcontinental highway was on his route to work.

Part 1

CHAPTER ONE

In The End

by Roland

This begins with the fact that what you are about to read in this part of the book is real; it did happen as reported and was witnessed by doctors, nurses and a family member.

It all begins on a chilly afternoon on a hill in Thunder Bay. We had rented our farm and moved into town to work in an Italian parish, St. Anthony's. I was on my way home from another day of teaching at a local high school. Climbing up the steep hill with walls of snow on either side, I noticed an occasional, sharp pain in my chest, which eventually dissipated upon resting for a few minutes. After five separate stops to recover, I made it through the front door of our home.

Very strange…what was that all about?

I did not think too much more about it for that night; however, that all changed the next morning (the statistical numbers on the most common time of a heart attack are early morning). I got out of bed with excruciating chest pains, sweating, nausea and dry heave vomiting. (*At that time, I did not know it, but these are the classic signs of a heart attack*). When I hit the floor at the top of the stairs outside my bedroom, our youngest daughter helped me up and insisted that we should drive to the closest hospital only two blocks away.

1

(*This is the point of a serious caution about what to do next with a suspected heart attack.* **Never** *drive yourself or allow someone to take you. You need medical help immediately.* **CALL FOR AN AMBULANCE**.….. *TO SAVE YOUR LIFE.*)

Of course, being in denial that anything was wrong, I thought it was too much trouble. (*A couple of months previously, my EKG and stress test confirmed that I had no problems related to any heart or artery issues.*) After all, I was only fifty years old.

The piercing chest pains continued to increase without relenting, and when we reached the doorway of the Emergency Department, I stumbled through the electric doors and fell on the floor! Staff and our daughter rushed to pick me up and put me on a gurney. Hospital alert codes were broadcasting in the halls and a group of medical staff gathered around the gurney. The cardiac signals on the heart monitor in the Emergency Room were very audible, and I was soon surrounded by three nurses and an two ER doctors.

Under the intensely bright lights, distressed voices were shouting out orders in rapid succession. Soon there were more medical staff in the small room already crowded with medical apparatus, and the orders became quicker and louder. More oxygen, etc.! (*I later found that there were an increased number of people in the room, because the night shift had stayed to help the changeover to the day shift. Very peculiar to me at the time were scissors which cut away all my clothes instead of just slipping them off? Obviously, time is of the essence with heart failure and imminent death.*)

As you can tell, by this time at the event I was very aware of all my surroundings, and that I was in serious heart attack trouble. The realization also struck me that our daughter's call to my dear wife, Erin, had gotten her off a shift in a surgery unit in a nearby hospital.

At this tense moment I saw the cardiac monitor, which visually and audibly recorded my heartbeat as it plummeted to a straight line, producing an alarming, steady whirring sound. It must be emphasized that this was not a sensational out of body experience or ADE (after death experience). I was watching everything with my own eyes and listening with my ears from the operating table. One nurse gasped… **"not breathing**," another choked out…**"no heartbeat."** The steady

whirring sound was followed by the most terrifying sound of all! One of the ER docs said in diminished voice,
   "We lost him."

I was clinically dead!

(*I would like to have interviewed the staff later about their impressions of all that happened that fateful day when my heart stopped, but that was not to happen.*)
   Erin's stealth entry visibly caused the ER staff some concerns, as she was in her scrubs but not one of the official staff with the security tag of that hospital. The strange appearance at the time was also accentuated by her boldly placing her hands over my heart. I was able to put my hand over hers in what I thought was a final goodbye embrace as I was slipping away. As if that was not enough, during all the shouting and medical devices, the room fell totally silent as the steady beeping of the monitor was replaced by a fixed whirring sound. She was praying in tongues—*Glossiola*, one of the gifts of the Holy Spirit, as recorded in Scripture. *And they were all filled with the Holy Spirit and began to speak in other tongues, as the Spirit gave them utterance.* (Acts 2.4).
   The ministry of Jesus Christ and his apostles included praying over the sick for healing and even over the dead to be brought back to life! At this moment Erin did not break down into weeping over the medical evidence........ she was praying over her dead husband. This was the ultimate action of faith in waiting on God!

Under these circumstances one would think that panic would be more in order at the thought and sight of my death; however, all that occurred was silence, peace and calm. To this day, we do not know how long the time was that my heart stopped, and Erin can only remember praying over me. There were no flashes of light, sounds or sweet aromatic scents.

There was only silence, peace and calm.

I woke up some time later with Erin as my first sight. I was moved to an intensive care unit with the now too familiar sound of the cardiac monitor proceeding at a reasonably steady pace with no stopping or alarms. I would remain there for five days and then be moved to a Telemetry floor with a *Holter monitor* (a mobile EKG) strapped to my chest for monitoring the condition of my heart from another floor in the hospital. Additional time in intensive care is standard hospital procedure because a second attack is typically expected within days!

The only comedy in this tragic part of my story is what happened next. The small electronic device, with at least eight wires taped to various parts of my chest and strapped to my body, had a small battery-powered red light that was slowly growing dimmer and dimmer until it finally disappeared. By the clock on the wall, it took twenty-five minutes for a nurse to rush into the room and check and see if my heart had stopped after it was finally noticed from another floor. I said, "It looks like I died twenty-five minutes ago, and it sure was nice of you to check on my corpse."

After a red face and convincing apology, she replaced the eight new batteries that are supposed to be dependable and "keep on running." All was well for a while...until the same scene was repeated and then three more times over the course of several days. When I was finally discharged from the hospital, I did thank the staff for my good care with an honest sentiment of gratitude. When relatives, friends and colleagues asked me about my recent heart attack, I had to confess that I "died" five times...once for real and four more times because of battery failure.

Getting back to the true story of a *dead man watching*, my survival was and remains to this day...a *miracle!* Our son in law was a resident in Medicine at that time, and Erin sent my hospital records to him for his consultation about what had happened. The medical record was shared with cardiologists on staff there, and their responses were significantly similar. The consensus was "there is no way this patient survived the magnitude of this heart attack."

The medical description of my event included an anterior cardiac artery completely blocked, resulting in a myocardial infarct (MI) to 35 % of my lower heart muscle. The Italian translation reads *mortadella or* "dead meat." My medical records show that the bottom of my heart is scar tissue and, according to present day medical science, will not function again.

Thanks be to God, to this day I have not experienced the typical heart pains under stress (angina), requiring the use of *nitroglycerin* that could become a daily routine for heart attack survivors. I did the research in preparation for seminars to be presented to a system-wide staff of aging teachers. The resulting seminars provided some scary statistics. In forty-five percent of all heart attacks, the ***first real sign of heart disease*** and/or atherosclerosis (plaque in the arteries) is **DEATH**! Medical science has moved far past my remote northern town

5

experience. Today more sophisticated methods are available to help with diagnosis and treatment of coronary arterial diseases.

Consequently, we remain thankful on an hourly basis for the blessing of a healthy heart life for many years. There was the statistical risk of a second episode within the same year. The actual date of this episode was long ago in winter, and it has been 26 years without another heart attack since the original event.

Another blessing of this story is the fact that after many years there have repeatedly been opportunities to witness to what God has done in my life. One recent event involved a meeting with two Orthodox nuns, while shopping in a grocery store. After some pleasantries I shared some of my story. After listening intently, they looked at each other, whispered a few words and agreed that I should change my name! "It should be 'Lazarus'." This scene has been repeated several times in different settings.

It has occasionally been a question in my mind, as to what Lazarus would have said about his experience of death. (*I am sure that he was eager to share his remarkable story with anyone who would listen.*) Unfortunately, little is said about Lazarus after he miraculously walked out of his tomb after being dead for four days. The Bible records that many people from the surrounding area came to see him and to hear his story His sister was upset with Jesus for showing up too late and warned Jesus that Lazarus would stink with the corruption of death. *Lord, by this time there will be an odor for he has been dead four days.* (Jn 11.39)

Because psychological and emotional stress is often identified as a major catalyst for heart disease, I was advised that I should go on medical leave for some rest and relaxation. We moved to the home we already owned in the Southwest US. With family and friends there, it truly was a time to regroup and set up a new course. My pension was moved up without penalty, thanks to legal help and support from friends in *Mended Hearts* (a hospital heart recovery group). As a result, we were blessed with an income, which freed us from being concerned about living expenses.

Looking back on how that evolved is another sign of God's mercy in my life. Too often a medical disaster is combined with the follow-up financial catastrophe. At the time we had one entering university and one in high school, while the other five were setting out on their own adventures, including missionary work, further schooling, and even professional football. We were very blessed to have an income and the time to deal with all the family progress and varying needs.

CHAPTER TWO

Extreme Stress. The cause of my death?

The back story to this first heart attack was very closely linked to the impact of stress on my life. The definition of heart disease can best be understood when read as *dis-ease*. While still teaching at the high school level with a master's degree, I had the opportunity to take a sabbatical leave for the purpose of graduate study abroad. I already had a master's degree in education, so my lifelong dream was to get a doctorate. *What a mistake that would turn out to be!*

The first step was to apply to a university. With the graduate record and entrance exams completed, we were ready to pick up and move the family two thousand miles to the "scene of the crime." All this was done without first investigating the department and the faculty. I have found after many conversations with scholars, holding earned doctoral degrees, that my case was not at all rare.

After the successful completion of the program requirements, the real obstacle started with the department head. He had been at my defense presentation and verbally approved the work; however, this positive affirmation was to radically change. In a few days. He called me into his office to announce that my dissertation document was "not acceptable." When asked what made it so, his answer was presented as a challenge. Either I change my dedication page, or the dissertation would not be advanced to the graduate dean for acceptance, publication and the granting of the degree. His issue was the simple statement that did not include gratitude for him or any member of his department. It simply read:

"THANKS BE TO GOD"

It had become politically correct behavior for academics in modern America to categorize and treat Christians as ignorant, superstitious and unscientific, while color, gender perversion and occult religions are not to be criticized or held up to ridicule for any reason.

My final word of advice for all who think they might want to pursue a Ph.D. is presented here with heartfelt conviction. *Be careful about where you apply and be sure to travel to the university to investigate into what you are about to invest your time, money and perhaps more. Don't blindly sign up because you succeed in the application process. Once you begin the huge investment, you are trapped, with only your good intentions.*

CHAPTER THREE

After the End

All was well and good for many years after that heart attack and completion of the doctorate: the graduations, the weddings, the grandchildren born adding to the family number. At the time of the writing of this book there were 23 grandchildren in all. Praise the Lord!

After a few years in Canada, we returned to the USA to spend our golden years in retirement in the sunny, warm Southwest. I received a surprise invitation to the Graduate School of Education in a small Christian college out West. That episode was another strange twist in this story. Erin and I were flown out to interview and meet with college administration and faculty. The process concluded after three intense days of interviews. Keep in mind that it was very clear that I am a Catholic and this was a Protestant university. When the provost challenged me, along with some others about the Reformation and what I had "missed." I simply answered, "Let's not go there."

At the conclusion of three intense days, we found ourselves sitting in a large circle of staff and administration with about fourteen people. After a few more questions, the provost had a pivotal question for me. "After all of our questions of you, do you have any questions for us?" Without hesitation or consulting Erin, I confessed my real response…one you should never give at a job interview. Remember, I already had a good income from my pension, so I didn't really need the professorship. I simply said, "Would all of you make my life much easier and not offer me this position on your faculty of Education." All conversation ceased...abruptly. After a sustained period of silence and some courteous farewells, everyone got up and left the room.

When we exited the door, we both glanced at each other with big smiles and silently agreed ...that would be the last we would hear from them. But God had another plan. We left to take a plane back to our home where we received a surprise call from the Dean of Education. To my amazement, she offered a full professorship with one year of tenure and potential for permanent tenure.

This was an impressive offer in academia for a new hire. Rather than accept on the phone, I said we would consider their generous offer and pray about it. We prayed about it and received the answer that I should take the position.

I had recovered from the heart attack trauma and was looking forward to training secondary teachers. So, we packed up again and moved to our new home in northern California. The job benefits lasted for four years and provided for our youngest daughter's bachelor's degree. Our youngest son finished high school there, and he met the person who would eventually become his lovely wife. Erin and I are convinced that the job had more than one purpose: he had to meet and fall in love with the girl he would marry. *We know that in everything God works for good with those who love him, who are called according to his purpose. (Rom 8.28)*

At this time, the largest single group of our family was residing in Canada. We chose a geographic location close to all three families, and our new residence was established there.

In the following years there began a new phase in our retirement, living in a beautiful, little home in SW Florida purchased by our oldest son. There were winter stays of four to six months per year. We began to lead two lives--each with family, friends and Christian communities. It was a blessing for fifteen years to be able to spend cooler summers up North and warm winters in the southern part of the United States as "Snowbirds."

Part 2

CHAPTER FOUR

Are you going to take my life now, Lord?

All went well until one early September morning in our Canadian home. I got out of bed only to collapse on the floor unable to get up.

I know I'm not dead but why can't I move?

Erin rushed upstairs to see what happened when she heard the thump on the floor above. Her RN training identified my problem as a stroke: *sudden paralysis/numbness on one side of the body (mine was the left side), drooping on one side of the face, confusion, trouble speaking, etc.* An ambulance and paramedics were at our door within minutes.

With signs of stroke or heart attack--call an ambulance, *as time is crucial for treatment. Also, if exact time of the event can be verified, this will determine whether the patient might qualify for a clot busting drug...I was ineligible for this intervention because the timing was unclear.*) The US statistics on deaths per year caused by heart attacks and strokes are over 650,000. (www.CDC.gov.). This informative website contains many other helpful directions to learn more about cardiovascular health.

We were off for another trip to the ER, where the CT scan of my brain showed a massive *Right hemisphere stroke* presumed to have been caused by a total carotid artery blockage. A subsequent MRI revealed two halves of my brain, which was black on one side and completely white on the other (saturated with blood). The stroke was so massive that one half of my brain appeared dead.

Our seven married children dropped everything and flew thousands or drove hundreds of miles to be with us. Not an easy task with all those grandchildren left behind and with only one parent in charge of the busy lives that required a team effort daily.

At the time my brain functions were so wobbly that I just said, "Hello," to each as though they just dropped in from across the street.

Our son, the fireman with paramedic training, stayed the first night at my bedside and found what was later identified as one of the probable causes of my stroke. During the night I stopped breathing several times. He simply used his pro football strength to lift and turn his 220-pound dad over so he could continue breathing. The younger son had night number 2 and panicked when the same thing happened. This time his desperate call for help produced what I thought was very strange the next morning. I woke up with oxygen tubes in my nose.

Sleep Apnea, a condition caused by a collapsed airway, had forced stress on my heart and arteries. This was the probable cause of the massive stroke. (*For people who snore loudly: be aware. You could have sleep apnea and need a* **CPAP**--*a Constant Pulmonary Airway Pressure device.) to help prevent a future stroke.*)

The staff neurologist at that time spoke with Erin privately and he was quite puzzled that I had even survived, given the magnitude of the blockage and subsequent brain damage. Our firefighter son brought some cutting-edge ideas about onsite stroke reversal, so I was immediately swallowing quantities of what I guessed might be WD-40, the spray lubricant I used for many decades on cars and household jobs.

Swallowing the expensive Norwegian fish oil, that one of our daughters immediately bought, became part of my recovery. Amazingly, after a lot of prayer to Jesus Christ, offered by many, and only ten days in the hospital, I returned home in decent shape: *walking, talking and chewing gum all at the same time*! When we left the hospital, I was curious about two of the many people in my ward that were in wheelchairs with withered hands, head down and unable to move. Erin quietly informed me in the car ride home that they had both been there for several months following their similar strokes. As a result, I remain very thankful for the healing I experienced.

The only residual impairments of the stroke were my sense of taste and problems with music--both *right hemisphere* functions. The sense of taste disorder was discovered with the nurse's first attempt to see if I could swallow successfully. The effects of a stroke can impede the ability to swallow and cause serious choking. I was asked to try some vanilla ice-cream, as the clinical observation proceeded. The only problem on my end was the taste I knew should be vanilla (*Even as you read this you can recall its distinct taste*). However, my big surprise was that it seemed to be a terrible trick...*was this actually diesel fuel?* The problem now remained, the hospital food was horrible; not because it was, but because my brain was mixing up all the signals and providing false information about the taste of the food on the tray. This malady continued for many months after leaving the hospital. I lost twenty pounds.

Thanksgiving Day comes in October in Canada, and for weeks I quietly prayed that my correct sense of taste would return. In the meantime, Erin was insisting that I eat everything I could. Prayer continued that normal taste would return for the wonderful, yearly Thanksgiving Day feast. This was the annual event at our daughter's country estate that several of our families enjoyed together. Unknown to all present at the time was the spectacular change that happened. On this exact day...the sense of taste was normal again! The turkey, dressing, mashed potatoes, gravy and cranberries all tasted wonderful. What a blessing!

What about musical ability? It had disappeared as the aftermath of the stroke. The day after returning home from the hospital stay, I took out the violin I had played well for decades to see if it could be played. Not only was holding the left hand on the fingerboard hard to do, but the memory of the tunes had completely evaporated. I tried a simple Brahms's lullaby we can all hum. No deal. I tried to whistle it, thinking it was just the muscles in my left hand and arm. *What a disappointment!* Despite my best efforts it was not to be done. To this day I struggle to get a tune out of my violin and at church try to sing the hymns with some success.

CHAPTER FIVE

I can't believe this is happening again!

Life went on with good medical test results for several years, with one exception of another medical challenge in the fall of 2015. This time Erin and I were fixing supper and I could hardly believe what happened next. The sudden chest pain that was all too familiar from decades earlier. We took the first precaution (**With signs of a heart attack it was recommended then to chew on an aspirin asap.**) Again, an ambulance was at our door in a few minutes. (*Remember this: Call 911 for an ambulance!*)

Back in an ER. This time the technology had advanced to cardiac angioplasty to clear out plugged arteries or place a stent. My arterial system was filled with a dye used for imaging to insert a catheter. The cardiac arteries were entered with a stent (a stainless-steel mesh implant used to hold a blocked artery open). As I watched the screen and the tool entered the heart area, I heard the doctor's surprised exclamation as my initial prognosis was a large clot in one of my coronary arteries. "There's nothing there!" exclaimed the doctor. My audible response was "Praise the Lord!"

Early the next day in a perplexed mood, the cardiologist entered my intensive care room. "I could hardly sleep last night thinking about your images, so I rushed in this morning to review them for any error I might have made." Our only other contact with him was when Erin and our daughter got onto the same elevator he was riding. He could only say that my case was a total mystery to him, and he had never in all his years as a cardiologist seen a clot "spontaneously" dissolve. Does it sound more like a miracle and not "mystery?" I remain thankful for surviving yet again and remain a formerly *dead man watching.*

CHAPTER SIX

Believe it or else. Another End

That was not the end of that episode. After several days at home, I began to have excruciating abdominal pains. They were so intense that it was obvious that something was seriously wrong. I had to leave the room when our granddaughter was visiting us to keep from distressing her with all my pain. It was unrelenting pain for hours, worse than both heart attacks, pain that would not stop sitting or lying down. We were off to the ER again.

Bursting in the door with a demand for "morphine," I was told that was not going to happen. After telling me to calm down for a checkup with no pain killer, it was determined that my urinary system had shut down and was careening toward kidney failure--the typical herald of death. Was this a reaction to the dyes used for the cardiac images a week earlier?

A whole new set of problems started to unfold. After draining a huge amount of fluid out of my bladder via a Foley catheter, it was determined that an MRI (magnetic resonance imaging) would provide some answers. Once completed, the images indicated a large mass in my bladder. Then the urologist informed us with the bad news about an observed and recorded bladder tumor. A scheduled cystoscopy would happen as an outpatient within days. The procedure is to insert a camera with light into the bladder from the front to remove a small amount of tissue for a biopsy. The scene and message of potential doom were all very businesslike.

The next step was to get the results from my personal MD. He opened with words you never want to hear after a biopsy session with a specialist.

"Roland, I wish I had better news for you."

He stated that the large mass in my bladder was determined by a radiologist, and confirmed by the oncologist, from its content and appearance to be cancerous.

The typical protocol would have to be surgery to completely remove my bladder with the tumor and replace it with a reconstruction using a section of your intestine. *Oh, no! It sounded like I would get to be a urological Frankenstein.* As if that wasn't enough, there was his additional threat that "the cancer may have already spread to lungs and nearby organs or even your brain."

I left that meeting in tears, facing my potential death. When I finally made it through the parking lot to our car, I told Erin we might have to start making plans for my funeral, including the purchase of a coffin.

We began a campaign of calls to the same urologist for when this *life-* saving *surgery* could take place. Weeks of calling without answers raised our anxiety levels to desperation. When we finally got an office clerk to give us a possible date, it would be months away because of his heavy, surgical schedule.

I called the urologist I had seen a few times in Florida to describe the unfolding disaster in Canada, as I was already being treated by him for repeated UTIs. He said what is nearly comical compared to the Canadian program, "Come in this afternoon." That would be rather difficult to accomplish as we were calling from Canada. We bought flight tickets for Sunday, and we were in his office by Monday.

He discretely indicated, "We need to take a look at this again." He had already received all my medical records from the Canadian urologist, including images and the need for surgery as soon as possible. He did not repeat the unwelcome threats about "wishing he had better news". We were back in his office for another cystoscopy on Wednesday of the same week. By this time, I was very clear about how it all worked. The camera was used again for the look around to confirm the size and location of the suspected cancer mass in my bladder. After years of teaching photography in high school and universities, I was puzzled by his technique.

He continued to circle around and look at the same areas several times. At the end of this intense period and anxiety for Erin and me watching the same screen, we heard the urologist's conclusion. Audibly surprised, he exclaimed, "There's nothing there!" This was the identical phrase used by the cardiologist when looking for a clot in my cardiac arteries. What are the chances of the exact same phrase being repeated?

Great relief was followed by his unexpected admission. The surgery he had already booked was cancelled. He had started the process to do what the Canadian urologist had recommended in his notes but did not do. One might be tempted to think that my records were switched or incorrect…or that *Jesus had healed me again* on the flight. Our children and friends, Anita and Edwin, along with many others had prayed fervently for my healing, and we accepted a prophetic word from Anita that this was "just a bump in the road." Well, the "bump" had absolutely *disappeared*. Praise Jesus!

Once again, I had escaped a disaster by God's mercy. What else can be said? The prescribed surgery in Canada might have been done needlessly and the medical records might have simply read "no cancer was removed."

How can I keep from singing and praising God!

For the first few years after the first life threatening incident, my anxieties were so great that trying to talk about it typically ended in tears. I would get so choked up that all people could do was feel sorry for me, only leaving me far short of my goal, which was to praise and give thanks to God for His mercy and healing in my life.

The writing of this book has taken over twenty-five years to get up the courage to put it all together. You have not been able to see the many times I have had to stop writing for a good cry. I could only start again "in illegible code," because my fingers were once again in the wrong positions on the keyboard.

As of the time of this writing, I remain in God's hands with relatively good health. My urinary system is free of cancer but is still in need of healing, not uncommon for a seventy-five-year-old man, let alone a previously *dead man.*

Part 3

CHAPTER SEVEN

My Life Goes on In Endless Song

At this stage the question is very appropriate.

Why was my life spared, not once, but several times?

The major clue is to go back to the question of why did Jesus save Lazarus? His name means *God helps*. A simple review of that dramatic salvage of a human life can best be explained by his relationships. First, he was Jesus' friend and the brother of Martha and Mary. The story involves His arrival too late to save Lazarus. We find Martha lamenting her brother's untimely death. She questions Jesus about why he didn't show up earlier-- before Lazarus died. *Lord, if you had been here my brother would not have died.* (Jn 11.21) The answer was to demonstrate the glory of God. *I am the resurrection and the life; though he dies, yet shall he live....* (Jn 11: 25) To this day it has been my realization that the pivotal person in my being a *dead man watching* my own death is and always will be... *Erin*.

She was the Martha that prayed to God to spare and revive my life. I honestly believe that had our dear daughter not been able to get Erin to come to the hospital that fateful day to pray for me, I might have been dead and soon buried.

Going back several hundred words is my reference to the amount of time it took for me to get up the courage to write this book. The only person who kept insisting for many years that I must write my story is our dear friend in Christ, David S. I took so long to start, because--as previously stated--it is a difficult topic with emotional memories that were painful.

If you want to completely halt the progress of a conversation in any context even after a church service, a family gathering, with friends or colleagues. Just ask this question:

So, what do you think about death?

You will not get a response. People usually do not and will not talk about this taboo subject. When was the last time you talked about death? It's not even a topic on the obvious occasion when it is the reason for a gathering--a ceremony, celebrated or grieved. You never hear the word "death" at a funeral. Today's society's code word is "passed." I know it is so obvious that you don't even want to read this brief challenge, *so let's drop the subject.*

In my case, I now know that my life has been spared so that I might become what is on the front page of this book: a witness to the mercy and power of God. How did that happen? The seed was planted with the Charismatic Renewal in the millennium to the Catholic Church and continues to spread to this day. This includes the gifts and power of the Holy Spirit we heard about from the pulpit, in the media and from Catholics and many other Christians everywhere.

We were presented with amazing opportunities that began to emerge in Canada and the USA. Remember that Erin and I had two separate lives. The one in Canada and another in Florida. Our Canadian Life included my hobby retirement job in southern Ontario as a classic car appraiser. It meant that to promote my insurance related business I drove a rare 1985 Mercedes 500 SL roadster to cruises and shows in the area.

A few years ago, I was inspired to change this otherwise decadent, materialistic celebration of the valuable cars driven to these shows by aging men in their sixties, seventies and even eighties. These men are reliving the dreams of their youth. They couldn't afford or get that car back in "the day," the '55 Chevy Blair convertibles, but now they are retired and have the time and money for their old favorite car. They drive around to show off their prize possession. Does that all sound a rather silly? Well, it really was, and when I finally realized that I was just another of the old guys bragging about my car, it was time to do something with the gift I had been given. As a grateful and revived dead man, I have the responsibility to witness to God's gift of life. This was the beginning of my journey that can best be called "fishing" at car shows. The first stage of fishing is to bait your hook. In my case this fishing ministry starts with something to catch the eye of the subject.

Unlike any other of the expensive large signs that are displayed at the front of the prized possession cars, my sign changed dramatically. Instead of just bragging about rarity, cubic inches and horsepower, my sign concluded with a totally unique statement. *This rare car was driven to this car show by a dead man.*

Me seated next to my Mercedes at a car show

I am always strategically seated in my lawn chair next to the front fender, watching as admirers of the car stop to read the plaque. Those who get to the bottom are at times visibly surprised to read the most important part of my sign. I see wives elbow their husbands, and then they both look at me puzzled. *There, I got a bite.* A few just read, look at the car and walk away. Most of the time they ask if this is my car, and if I am the man in the car plaque story. The catch has begun. There it is my opportunity to talk about the subject that no one ever wants to talk about: "death" and what happens after death.

The church going folks that stop are blessed by the testimony of God's mercy, as the plaque concludes. Some just ask about what it means. That's when it is time to get to work; it's my clue to ask a pivotal question. "Do you know where you are going next?" Their simple answer is typically, "to look at the rest of the car show." That is followed by the next stage. *No, do you know where you are really going next?* By this stage in my "going fishing" ministry, the typical answer is "I don't know." There it is... an opportunity to witness, as the red headed girl did in New York City.

My answer is a bold confession. "I know where I'm going. Do you want to know where you are going?" By this stage the navigation gets sensitive with a total stranger. It's time to fire off a quick arrow prayer for the Holy Spirit to guide me to the next and what might be my last statement. If they say, "How do you know where you are going?" My answer is about God's mercy and my confidence in what the Gospel is all about and clearly contains. *For the word of God is living and active, sharper than any two-edged sword, piercing to the division of soul and spirit, of joints and marrow, and discerning the thoughts and intentions of the heart.* (Heb 4.12) I have often had the opportunity to pray with people who start to open a little with stories about dying or dead relatives. The car plaque has worked as an effective bait and hook and this cold call has started the process.

Think about it! How many times in the past ten years has someone introduced himself as a "dead man" or asked you if you want to go to heaven or where your destination might or should be?

This has been all about how my "fishing" ministry typically

happens. I don't keep any records but simply expect in faith that many small conversations about God's love have or will at some point in the future have the intended impact. Sometimes I plant or harvest. *The Sower sows the Word.* (Mk 4.14)

Perhaps one of the most difficult cases was the sad and weary-looking, older owner of a rare Cadillac parked near my car. He stooped over and spent an intense period reading my plaque. He responded with some indignation. "So, what does this mean?" When I moved through my sequence of questions, he had a response I was not prepared for and never hoped to hear again.

"I'm going to hell!"

I was speechless. After a silent prayer, I could only whisper, because I was so grieved by his abrupt and serious condemnation of himself. The words of an old hymn started to emerge. "Softly and gently, Jesus is calling, come home, come home." Inspired, I entreated him, "Please sir, just pick up the phone." He slowly turned away without response.

That biblical story of the rich man and Lazarus (Lk 16.19-31) provides guidance for this situation. *…neither will they be convinced if someone should arise from the dead.* (Lk 16.31)

I could only pray that this encounter might cause him to reconsider what must be a desperate interior life without hope. The fishing ministry continued all summer with one or two classic car shows per week.

This man's wife stopped by a few minutes after he left to explain that her husband had been mad at God for decades and that he had terminal cancer and little time to live.

With tears in her eyes, she appeared the next year at the same annual car show to announce that her husband was alive and well and in remission. And, he had started attending church with her after many years of refusing. Praise God!

Leaving for the southern United States each November meant the end of the car show ministry and the completely different one in our American life. We had a great personal blessing there a few years ago when we met a special, dedicated couple from Indiana one Sunday after Mass. Denny and Margret Ann had been involved in Pro Life action for many decades, so they invited us to their "sidewalk ministry "in Ft Myers, praying to save little Americans from death by abortion every Tuesday and Thursday for approximately four to five hours each time.

Without this ministry we might be like millions of snowbirds that enjoy winters in the South at the beach or on the golf course, having fun in the sun. It is a blessing to be involved. We sit on the sidewalk in front of a death camp as real as Auschwitz in the early 1940's. We pray for God's mercy for the women in difficult and sometimes desperate situations who have come to have their own children murdered. There have been 911 calls made for medical help when a hemorrhaging, botched abortion victim in the back seat of a car is in a life-threatening condition. The abortionist and staff avoid the confrontation and bad publicity of a near or actual death resulting from their malpractice.

Erin is committed to helping moms say *yes to life* for their little ones. Along with several others who are very knowledgeable and prayerful, she is a sidewalk counselor for those in need of support in what is often a challenging and fearful time. Young mothers are provided with information about the lives of the babies within them and given material about medical help and many other avenues of assistance. The counselors stand near the driveway and hand out informative pamphlets and talk to those who are headed toward the abortion clinic. We keep records of those who come out and say they have changed their minds. Over the past years we have averaged a good number of lives saved per winter season. We can provide many with substantial assistance through ministries devoted to the care of both mother and child.

Pregnancy homes are in some cases a lifesaver. It is not just *"save your baby and go on your way as best you can."* Instead, these are well-functioning residences for young mothers who are commonly abandoned by their fathers, their friends and family and with no place to go. The pregnancy outreach in our city provides them, about twelve at a time, with complete housing, a free meal plan, training, education, babysitting and a clothing allowance. The stay is for two full years. The ministry costs about six thousand dollars per year per mother. The results are substantial. Some of the new moms are from difficult backgrounds with heartbreaking details. The opportunities at this outreach have provided very good results. One of the moms we met and talked with had completed her GED and gone through nurses' training.

This is why we tell friends and acquaintances in both countries that we get to go to *lifesaving* in Florida. The typical confusion about this description is that others think we are going to swimming classes. That is our opener for invitations to review another form of the *death taboo in our society... abortion.*

Awareness of the abortion industry in Canada and the USA is a topic not to be discussed at any time and particularly at church. Often people do not want to know what is going on, just like the German public did not want to know what the Hitler regime was doing in Auschwitz and Dachau.

This whole ministry is not without its challenges. One year the owner of the failing office complex in the low-income area, where the so-called "clinic" dedicated to "women's health" was located, tried to stop us.

What about the health and safety of the innocent child that would become another statistic in the death records? What about the physical, emotional, spiritual health and welfare of the woman, who would choose not to respect and protect her own child's life?

The owner had the police come to make us get off the public sidewalk. Pro-life activism is not welcome in the society and particularly with the pro-death and gender mixed-up administration in America and Canada in recent times. A national legal support team for pro-life people being harassed by organizations dedicated to abortion in America showed up to help us. The lawyers argued that we were not impeding traffic, as the police had charged, and that we had every legal right to be on the public sidewalk praying and speaking at the corner of the driveway. (It should be noted that the abortion clinic was distantly out of sight from where the counselors were stationed.) The plaintiff had to pay a substantial sum in legal fees and court costs, as ordered by the judge who had ruled the same way ten years earlier about the same issue! As far as we were concerned, the point was to make a just decision that had nothing to do with financial gain. Of course, it did not even reach the news in the local area. But we did win and as a result can continue lifesaving!

CHAPTER EIGHT

The list of Family Miracles

Believe it or else. There is a family tradition of close calls. Here are a few of our testimonies.

Our oldest daughter started out as very athletic and very much of a risk taker. After her first mission trip with a teen mission outreach, she went to work full time for that same teen missions' ministry. She traveled all around the globe, as she worked her way to an executive position that placed her in charge of thousands of teenagers each summer with trips to different countries on every continent.

She had so many stamps on the back of her passport that they had to add extra pages. Their evangelization methods included what are known from the Middle Ages as "mystery plays" in mime, notably the life, death and resurrection of Jesus Christ. She met renown people like Mother Theresa of Calcutta in India; she also met the converted tribal member who took part in the killing of 5 missionaries in the jungles of South America. Her experiences included being in an active war zone and dodging bullets and mortars in Nicaragua. She was even mugged on the streets in Morocco.

She narrowly escaped death in the African jungles from charging elephants, hippopotamuses and alligators. It sounds like I'm making this up, but I'm not. A most serious threat on her life was in 1988, the year that a nuclear reactor in Chernobyl, Russia, exploded into a meltdown and sent a radioactive cloud over northern Europe. Ironically, she had no idea of the disaster because the Russian government successfully delayed reporting the story in Europe. We encouraged her by phone to leave as soon as possible because of her proximity to Kiev in the Ukraine, the area which is still experiencing the deadly effects of the nuclear fallout.

Years later she married a successful Christian lawyer, and she and her husband are now raising three lovely children in Dallas Texas.

Our third daughter is also on the list of miraculous cures. While working in the USA at a large, interstate trucking company, we received an emergency call one cool day in January of 1993. It was our dear son-in-law. He and our third eldest daughter had just married that summer and were living in Ottawa while he was in residency at the University Medical Center. Remember him-- he was the doctor in training who showed my lethal heart attack records to cardiologists.

The call was to report that his wife/our daughter had been experiencing spells of blindness and debilitating migraines. The prognosis after tests and images of her brain was not good. They indicated the cause was a tumor the size of a walnut at her pineal gland in the very center of her head. The neurosurgeon's report was about a very delicate operation that could take as much as ten hours. The results of this brain trauma included the warning for them to be aware of the possible dire consequences of the operation. She could come out blind or deaf, or both. If unsuccessful, the operation could be fatal.

Within a few days we were in the waiting room praying for the success of the procedure by one of Canada's notable neurosurgeons. The waiting room had two other families in the same type of life-or-death situation. One was a motorcycle accident victim. His injuries later were to be the cause of his death. The other family had a similar concern about a brain tumor.

Her operation included entering her skull from the rear at the base to lift her brain to insert a metal tube about one inch in diameter so the tumor could be delicately extracted with forceps. (*Thank you, Lord Jesus, the biopsy was negative.*) What an answer to prayer! She survived and made it through well. The somewhat scary procedure included the insertion of a shunt, or drain tube, from the base of her brain down her neck to the top of her stomach to relieve fluid pressure from her cranium and would remain there to the present.

In the subsequent years since this traumatic episode, the couple have been blessed with their four multi-talented children.

The third and most recent family near death experience was also close to the dead man watching story and would be *Our Christmas Miracle of 2015.*

Our second daughter had been ill with terrible flu for several days when her husband found her unresponsive on the bathroom floor. With some difficulty she was rushed to a local hospital. The prognosis was bad.

We received her husband's call at our winter home on the gulf coast about one-hundred and eighty miles south of their suburban home. We presumed the call was about their plans to come to our house the next day for Christmas and the holiday celebration. The presents were under the tree and all the food was ready. What a shock to hear of her dire situation. We loaded up our van not knowing if we would arrive three hours later for a serious operation or the preparations for a funeral.

Her blood pressure had fallen to a low of 50 over 30... next to nothing. She had pericardial effusion (e.g., fluid around her heart), inhibiting its ability to pump. All this was happening on Christmas Eve. The difficulty in finding a cardiologist to deal with this life-threatening condition was quite serious. The next stage was a plan to send her by helicopter to a downtown hospital for help there from a competent specialist. That was delayed until the morning, and she was transported by ambulance to that hospital in Orlando.

The cardiologist was forced to do an emergency evacuation of fluid from the pericardium around her heart. Her heart had nearly stopped. He announced with alarm and no courtesy, "You're dying!" Sound familiar to "we lost him"? <u>He opened her chest through the sternum</u> to place a drainage tube as quickly as he could to remove the fluid that was seriously restricting her heart function. It was not the less invasive procedure that was originally planned, but it worked. Although barely living, she had survived. She left the hospital 5 days later in extremely weak condition, weighing only ninety-eight pounds.

We stayed a month to help with taking care of their three children. All the household chores and school pickup and drop off after the Christmas break was a reminder for Grandma and Grandpa of how much work, challenge and joy was involved with having a young and vibrant family (three children).

Their Christian community was very generous to bring over meal after wonderful meal, including a complete holiday dinner with all the trimmings on Christmas day. The children knew that mom was in the hospital without the awareness of the fact that she might never come home again.

For many days and nights all she could do was get out of bed to use the washroom. She was so weak after the medical trauma that recuperation would take several months. Erin stayed to help longer. She was full time RN, kitchen staff, chauffeur, house cleaner and day/night care for the kids. It was a lot of work, but it required intervening at a critical moment. Like the pivotal entry into the ER of her dying husband in Canada she was a needed blessing for all the family. Erin returned to our Florida home after several weeks, and we went back again to Florida Life and lifesaving together.

Our daughter took a long time with a lot of help and prayer to make it through the winter. By spring she could walk around her patio in the backyard. She recovered enough to apply for and get accepted to a graduate school program in Law late that summer. When starting a family, she had retired from Associate Dean of Arts & Sciences and was well qualified and blessed to get a generous scholarship. This was another lifetime dream that almost ended in death before it got started.

The fourth family miracle is the *hero*. We say this because he was in the news for his recognition by the mayor of his city. Our oldest son was the courageous firefighter who rescued two people in a burning convertible on his long drive home from our family reunion. At risk of an imminent explosion, he jumped out of the family van at the edge of the city to rip off the top of the convertible and pull out to safety the two crash survivors trapped in the car. All this time the front of the car was in flames and could have exploded at any minute. He would not tell us about this dramatic save, but his dear wife called to give us the news.

That was not the only event that year. He has always been involved in body building as part of his training through college football and pro ball in the CFL. But this could have all ended in another instant with a bad accident in a gym. Pulling against a lot of weight ended with a near death accident. Sitting and pulling backwards on hundreds of pounds ended when the cable snapped. The force sent him to the floor backwards to land at breakneck speed on his head.

We got his call from the hospital ER, as he went there with serious pains in his neck. The doctor told him he was lucky to even be alive after what should have been a broken neck, possibly resulting in a wheelchair for life. With physiotherapy and God's grace he recovered very well within a few weeks. The couple continue to raise their four beautiful children.

Our youngest daughter, the one who miraculously was able to get her father, who could barely walk, to the hospital during his heart attack, was part of a youth missionary outreach to India. There was a time of preparation before departing for India, in which the young people were confronted with questions relating to their upcoming journey. They were asked, "What would you do if you were asked to touch a leper? Their responses were generally positive and along the lines of willing to do so for Jesus. However, when she was asked, she responded, "No way!" as she was repulsed by the thought of touching someone infected with a contagious disease.

With excited anticipation, the mission outreach team finally arrived in Calcutta, India, intent on being witnesses to God's love and hoping to find opportunities to serve others. However, their enthusiasm was abruptly quenched when at the train station all their backpacks, including their money and passports, were stolen in broad daylight. This event caused them to be sequestered in a hotel, while the adult leader was trying to have the passports reissued and the stolen funds replaced. This took several days of intense effort.

In the meantime, she was becoming restless and decided she would venture out to find Mother Teresa's *Home for the Dying.* She set out alone in a dramatically different environment from what she was used to and after several disheartening wrong turns she finally reached the Home.

It was here that she offered to help in any way, such as feeding the residents, sweeping, washing floors, etc. A worker led her to a woman reclining on the floor and told her to hold her while washing her wounds and then help with some cloths that were provided. She did so, and as she proceeded to cleanse the sores, the worker passed by and said, "By the way, this lady has leprosy."

It must be noted that Father Damian (now Saint Damion of Molokai, a Catholic priest, had died of this same illness), when over a century ago he ministered and lived among Hawaiians who suffered with leprosy.

Our daughter did not contract the disease, but through this experience and many other notable ones, she concluded, "*I know that God is real!*"

The remaining family miracles include our children who have been in auto accidents in one place or another. The list starts with daughter #4, who is happily married with 4 children. Our #5 daughter, who is married to a youth pastor, has 3 children. And our youngest son, who is also now married with a couple of children had his memorable car accident when he was 14. In all the cases there were minor injuries but no fatalities.

A frequent quote from the past is that ***family that prays together, stays together***. And we all praise God that He has answered the many prayers offered at both peaceful and frantic times in our lives.

Rejoice always, pray constantly, give thanks in all circumstances; for this is the will of God in Christ Jesus for you. (1 Thes 5.17)

CHAPTER NINE

Long before my End

My life began as a child in the northwestern Ontario town that became the very same place of my death.

Oddly, this place no longer exists.

For Canada's centennial. Port Arthur was renamed Thunder Bay. In fact, I was born in the same hospital in which I later survived death. My comic line is that I was born and died in the same place, "nowhere." If that is not enough, I was baptized in the same Italian parish in that very town. After years of suffering through the freezing winters there, my parents decided it was time to move to better weather. As a result, my first couple of years of the mid 1940's was spent in Miami, Florida. Things changed again after one huge hurricane, and it was decided it was time to get out of town. We moved to the other US coast in sunny California. That lasted several years until my dad, the happy wanderer, decided we should move from California to a dry climate in the Southwest to relieve my mother's asthma. The city we settled in was the same one where I went through grade school, high school and my first university degree.

All was well for my first six years of life, until one night when I woke up screaming with pain in my legs. In a panic my mother did the only thing she could think of. She wrapped my legs with damp warm towels and then massaged them with much effort. I discovered shortly afterwards that I could barely stand and brace myself with a chair to get to our bathroom. I don't remember going to a doctor, but I guess my mother had been advised that her original method for relieving my pain was the best; and, in fact, it was the same technique that Sister Kenney had pioneered twenty years before in Australia. I had contracted **polio.**

Poliomyelitis is the highly contagious disease that was blamed on public swimming pools and its water-borne virus that was common throughout the USA. Dr. Jonas Salk developed his Nobel Prize winning Polio vaccine in the 1960's. Franklin Delano Roosevelt was too late for that treatment and spent most of his adult life with steel braces on his legs and in a wheelchair during his three terms as president. In my case, the disease which killed thousands and crippled many more throughout the world, did not have the same devastating effect.

After recuperating over a period of months, I did not know why I could not attend school or the secret of why I had to use crutches to get around. I am now left with the revelation that God started to redirect my life at a very early age. He continues to do so, hour by hour. My life goes on in endless song. How can I keep from praising?

Years later, after getting married and starting a family, Erin and I started working in that parish in northwestern Ontario where we learned about Fr. Carlo's Scalabrini Order. They are a group of Italian Priests whose ministry in the new world in the 19th century was to immigrant Italians in North and South America. Their 20th century mandate expanded to all immigrants to the New World. We were very inspired by the founding Bishop's mandate to the order of priests, "Even if all you do in your entire life as a priest is to save one person from hell, your ministry is worth your calling."

This is the point in the book for your piccolo Italian lesson. The words of an old Italian saying: *ieri, oggi, domani*. What does "yesterday, today, tomorrow" have to do with the whole theme of this book? As a survivor of polio, two heart attacks, a massive stroke and diagnosis of bladder cancer, I could be living in constant fear and depression. Fear that *yesterday's* medical record could be revisited at any moment because of clogged arteries and unpredictable recurrences. Fear, that *today* would be my final day of life. Or fear of tomorrow that death would come at an unwelcome time.

However, my trust is in Jesus Christ, who is the same *yesterday, today and forever* (Heb 13.8). He is as near as the mention of His Name. He is the Savior, the Healer, the Deliverer, the Provider. He is all we need. His promise is eternal life to all who turn away from wrongdoing, turn to Him for forgiveness and trust wholly in Him. His *perfect love casts out fear* (1 Jn 4:18).

> *Death is swallowed up in victory. O death, where is thy victory?*
> *O death, where is thy sting?*
> *(1 Cor. 15.55)*

> My life goes on in endless song.
> How can I keep from praising?

We trust these stories of how God's mercy has worked in our family might inspire the reader of this little book to consider that God is also calling you to trust in Him and accept His wondrous love.

Finally, the conclusion of our witness is found in the very last words of the Bible.

Maranatha

He who testifies in these things says, *Surely, I am coming soon. Amen. Come, Lord Jesus!* (Rev 22. 20)

CHAPTER TEN

At the last moment

At the last moment of completion of the first half of this book there was a surprising development in my terrible medical history.

As a requirement of prostate surgery in early 2017, a cardiologist verified that my damaged heart could endure the heavy sedation from the anesthesia required for the 2–3-hour procedure. After preliminary testing and confirming that it would be safe to proceed, the cardiologist also ordered an echocardiogram to review my heart condition.

The first heart attack survival 25 years earlier concluded with my survival and the medical prognosis that 35% of my heart muscle was dead (MI=myocardial infarct) and that my heart would for the rest of my life be working with the remaining 65% of the good tissue. My EF (ejection fraction) or the amount of actual pumping capacity was identified as <u>37% which is below normal.</u>

Following the updated test, the conversation with the cardiologist indicated that my numbers had undergone significant changes. The amount of previous MI was reconfirmed and identified as the same percentage however, my EF was estimated at <u>50% or within normal limits.</u> These are not changes that ever typically happen according to medical science. In fact, the typical trend is for these indicators of cardiac damage to remain constant or deteriorate with any subsequent events or simply the passing of time (i.e., getting old).

This time we got an answer to a prayer that was not even on our daily list. My heart condition and function has returned to what it probably was 30 years ago prior to my first massive heart attack and ER flat line episode. The cardiologist's complicated medical record of 4 pages of detailed numbers and ranges could have been included but the entire document can be reduced to:

Normal...............................Normal......................Normal.

Death is swallowed up in victory. O death, where is thy victory?
O death, where is thy sting? (1 Cor. 15.55)

My life goes on in endless Song.
How can I keep from praising and witnessing?

CHAPTER ELEVEN

Devastation of our home in 2022 and another Stroke and Near Death Again

In September of 2022, my midnight washroom break produced yet another scare. I could not walk without holding on to the walls. When I finally made it back to bed, I woke Erin up to tell her about the episode. I was able to get to sleep again but was in the ER again the next morning.

Off to the local hospital again. The first prognosis was vertigo. That progressed to a stroke in the Medulla (lower brain stem). Two unfortunate technical errors led to serious blood quantity problems. Again, I was in trouble in ICU. Watching the terror reports about an approaching hurricane.

For two days the local news reported widespread devastation from hurricane Ian in the Gulf area. The threats increased as the predicted landfall included Cuba and the West coast of Florida.

At 3:00AM the nursing help pushed my hospital bed into the hall for protection from flying debris and broken glass. There was a sudden commotion and yelling. Ian had made a direct hit on Ft Myers and Cape Coral! The news reports were of massive devastation and countless deaths and missing persons. Then, no more news...the electricity was out, and the water was out too. Weeks later the death count was over eight hundred. Once the power was on again the damage could be seen on TV with street after street where the entire contents of the houses were stacked in the front yard. Eventually FEMA trucks moved from one area to another using large grappling buckets to pick up the furniture, appliances, and cabinets along with clothes and bedding, etc.

Our saddest experience was to hear of an acquaintance whose body was found when the house was bulldozed like thousands of others. He had taken refuge in the attic.

My own sad story continued when the hospitals in Cape Coral and Fort Myers were damaged, flooded or closed! Our firefighter son came to the rescue again and drove me through multiple detours to meet our son-in-law who continued onto a hospital north of Orlando. The care and polite treatment there were in sharp contrast compared to the problems in the hurricane disabled hospital in Cape Coral. I saw a multitude of specialists; significant were the urologists who determined that my water system was impaired, as my prostate blockage was back to a rating of dangerous blockage.

The staff cardiologist determined that my damaged heart and exceptionally low hemoglobin number could not endure the stress of another operation. Following a blood transfusion, the staff anesthetist could successfully put me under for the three-hour operation called a TURP (i.e., Transurethral Resection of the Prostate).

Following anxious hours of waiting and multiple cancellations, I was finally wheeled through endless hallways to the scene of the procedure. I woke up to find Erin by my side, with a big smile, "it was a success!" despite the many problems with my clinical history. The transfusion that was done earlier resulted in the necessary rise in my hemoglobin (7 to 12) so the surgeon could do his work. The amazing blessing at this Christian hospital was a staff that commonly and daily prayed with patients. Each shift brought in new personnel and more stories of God's mercy. My stay was five weeks.

During that time, a lot of reconstruction was done at our home in Cape Coral. The first stage was to move out all the ruined furniture and cabinets to the front yard and then clean up the floors. The first to fly into help were the lawyer from Dallas and the Psychotherapist from Ontario, Canada. This was precious and valuable time sacrificed to help in the disaster in Florida. To start with they both had to wear expensive hazmat suits donated by generous relatives in Dallas. The house was so nasty, due to salt water and sewer-like canal mud. There was no water or electricity at that time. As a result, shovels and brooms were the only tools. Mold became the big enemy, and it required cutting the walls open 3 feet above the floor to disinfect and then replaster.

Our eldest son repainted the entire house inside when all the plaster and texture work was completed. He had two other houses in our area to deal with simultaneously. He completely refinished their rental, which needed extensive repair. Our youngest son formulated the plans and ordered all new kitchen and bathroom cabinetry for our house. The older son and the reconstruction team installed them, better than the originals. Our son dragged filthy water-soaked carpets out into the yard. Underneath was the original terrazzo. Afterwards our son spent six hours with a heavy machine to polish them, and the results were again better than before the hurricane. It is important to add that his wife (our daughter-in-law) has been very supportive and actively assisting in the clean up after hurricane disaster.

In addition to all the prayers, multiple family members were supportive and industrious, attending to every need. (We were very spoiled and profoundly grateful for everything.)

After Christmas, family members showed up for a reunion, which included a cleanup workday at our house. Our children and grandchildren committed to cleaning and repairing countless jobs throughout the interior. The house is now better than before the hurricane with the new roof and replaced gutters and fence around our pool.

What a blessing!

On the last week of my stay in Orlando a unique opportunity arrived in my private room as a young male tech with an uncommon hospital badge entered my room. His name was Mohammed. I opened our first brief encounter with a question about his nametag and if as I guessed he was a practicing Muslim? His quick defensive response was that he and his Imam were nonviolent, law-abiding citizens and not like the radical murderers on many TV news stories. My bold response was to ask him to investigate the history of his religion and mine. After he admitted that he had never seen a forbidden Bible, I told him I have a copy of the (Quran) Koran in English and had read and studied most of it, as retired professor at a Christian university with many friends in the Theology department.

I did not labor the last of the 5 pillars of the Koran (Jihad): *convert to Islam or die! Compare this to the Gospel message of love your enemies; repent, reform and receive the Good News.*

Christians have the Bible and One God (the Trinity with Father, Son and Holy Spirit). The Son was born of Mary and lived a human life of preaching, teaching and healing. He then was crucified, died and was buried to rise again on the third day to be with the Father.

Muslims have the Koran as their holy book dictated by an angel to the illiterate Mohammed about Allah--the vengeful and demanding god--with Mohammed as its founder who started a lifetime campaign of war and killing against the infidel (i.e., anyone that does not believe in Allah).

I asked him what the status of both founders would be if alive today? He looked puzzled by this uncommon question. I said that" if Jesus Christ was on earth today, He would be accepted by many but denounced by others as unstable for claiming to be God. If Mohammed was alive today, he would have some followers but reside in a federal penitentiary after being arrested and convicted of child rape; his first wife Aisha was recorded as being 6 or 7 years old when he took her in as his wife (consummated when she was only 9) along with many others!"

Mohammed had no comeback. I prayed that I had not been too forceful. I reminded him that the one outstanding common position of both religions is the pro-life stance on abortion and the emphasis on prayer.

His duty lasted a week, so he came in several times per day. My last question of him was, "where is the founder of each religion now?"

"I have no idea."

Well," according to the Bible, Jesus is alive and seated at the Right Hand of God the Father in Heaven. Your Mohammed is a pile of dust somewhere in the deserts of Arabia." And according to Muslim history, there would be a long battle over who would be his successor... Sunni or Shiite tribes.

The conclusion of his shift times, he thanked for the lessons and said he would seriously consider what I had told him about the critical differences between our religions. He must have gone back to his Imam with questions about the lessons. Could this be a time for planting? My hospital stay ended with a celebration of my recovery with staff applause and heartbreaking wishes for my return home.

We returned to our home to find our (new old) home and remain blessed and healthy to this date and beyond. Summer 2023.

How Younger Family Members Responded to Death

Hanna's Tribute to Her Great Grandmother

A most beautiful story someone could possibly write about the death of a loved one was written as a school literature project by the author's thirteen-year-old granddaughter in 2019. I include it here as a touching memoir of a response to the death of her great grandmother.

Memoir, April 5, 2019

In everyone's life, there are years that they feel they will always remember because of an especially significant growth or change that they went through. Though I am young, and have not had many years to compare with, I feel that this school year especially has had many things in store for me to learn. It has been so eventful, exciting, strange, confusing and upsetting, but I know it will be one of which I will always remember, look back on, and see how it has impacted my understanding of many things, and how God was shaping me.

We moved to Albuquerque in the spring of 2015 to take care of our elderly great grandmother, Ann, who lived with my great uncle, and were our only family members living in the city. Every Sunday after Church, we would drive to her little cozy house. We would come into the driveway, either arguing, upset, overjoyed, or just comfortable. Whatever our family had to worry about only lasted until we entered through her squeaky front door, for as soon as we walked in, we were carefree of the troubles outside the walls of her house. "We're here!" my mom would say in a tone not quite yelling, not quite soft - the perfect tone for my grandma to hear. Passing through the lifeless kitchen, we would collect the treats waiting in a jar on the counter, and then sneak into the den. All the toys that we had grown up with when we visited her, and played with tirelessly, were still there in the corner as they had always been; nothing ever changed. It was quiet beside the low volume of the television, and the slow, tranquil movements of my grandma. She would not know that we were there until we all greeted her with hugs and kisses. "Hi Grandma!" we exclaimed as we excitedly shuffled to a spot that she could see us. "Oh, hi!" she would say as a smile lit up her big blue eyes and her frail face. We hugged and kissed her. As we found our spots on the couch to watch TV with her, she would ask us questions about how we were, or comment on the TV show we were watching. When my mom made it to the den, she would greet Grandma the same way we did, and then help her to the kitchen to eat. There they would chat and my grandmother would tell her stories of all her extravagant travels, and we would often hear my grandmother laugh hysterically, reflecting on her wonderful life. She was so wise and such a sweet lady. I remember her as an old-fashioned doll, or a photo album of the best events in history. In her old age, she was such a bright light to everyone, even when she would just sit in a chair smiling up at everyone, with both her hands rested on the top of her cane. I am so thankful for this time, however, I wish that I had used this opportunity to ask her more questions about life situations, because I know that she would have been flattered, and I would have found her advice very helpful.

It was after one of the school soccer games that we went to visit her. We stepped up to the door, rang the doorbell, and after a while, she answered. She had tears in her eyes, spoke in a low voice, and was trembling. My mom and I were immediately struck with sadness as this was the most miserable we'd had ever seen Grandma. We came in and she informed us that her doctor had visited her and told her that her time to go was soon. We doubted her, but she seemed hopeless, and convinced us that, after 97 years of life, she was ready. The next month or so was a blur of soccer games, school, homework, and visiting

Grandma as often as we could. She was now limited to the chair in her room, and her bed. We now would find her sitting comfortably in her rocker with her head laid back and the lamp softly shining on her. She wore a smile and her eyes were closed. It was like she was talking to God face to face and it warmed my heart to see her so happy.

One day, I remember I sat with her for a while, while she was awake. She asked me how school was and I told her about my joys with my friends. After I had told her all of the fun times in the school year so far, she paused and slowly told me to keep my friends close because they were good ones and how she remembered her high school friends. Sitting there, I began to think about how far she had come, how many people she had met and affected, and it comforted and helped me to see life with new and more hopeful eyes.

Another month and my grandma slowly became wearier and stayed stationary in her bed. She was no longer able to speak. Our other relatives came to help take care of her.

I slowly and lightly snuck into her room one day to see her sleeping as usual. I felt a calling to sit and pray with her, and that is what I did. By her side, and holding her soft, elderly hands, I prayed, thanking God for this precious woman's life, love, and light. It was so quiet in the familiar air of her room, and I felt that for the hour that I was there, it was not just me and her. God was there with us, by her side, smiling down at her like I was.

Another month and we visited quietly time and time again, watching and praying for her. Her breathing became more and more labored and I knew that it was almost time for her to meet God. She looked like she was in more and more pain with every breath.

It was now the fall break and we were ready for balloon fiesta. We went to bed early in anticipation for the mass ascension the next morning. I was awoken very early, but it was not for the reason I expected. I looked up at my mom who had tears in her eyes, and tears immediately filled mine. "She is finally released," I thought. My mom and I hugged, and before I knew it, we were all at Grandma's house. The lights were dim and the house was still. It was silent besides quiet weeping and soft and sad voices on the phone. I was not sure that I wanted to see her without life in her eyes, but I had seen her in so much pain, that I decided to see her one last time along with my siblings. There she was, so frail, and lifeless, and still. Tears filled my eyes even more as each of us laid our hand on her - first Zach, then Joel, then Angelica, and last, me. I struggled to lift my hand, but I finally laid it on her shoulder, and the most amazing thing happened. I felt a rush of pure joy come through my hand and fill my entire body. A smile stretched uncontrollably across my crying face. I was no longer sad, because the happiness of heaven touched me for a split second. In that moment, I knew she was with God and felt more love and joy than she ever felt while she was living. I contemplated about life and death. I realized that life is such an amazing gift, but it does not compare to seeing the face of God. She lived her life well and inspired me with hope and taught me to love. She would always say that when we would visit her, that we made her day, but it was really she who made our day. It is a beautiful thing to share your life or just a fraction of it, with someone else, to help them, while also being extremely affected by that person. We have such an amazing gift from God; his love and mercy. But not only that, he has given us the ability to love for his glory.

My hand slowly slid off her shoulder as I kissed her on the forehead, and slowly left with tears in my eyes, a smile on my face, and the love of God in my heart.

Marla's Message to Her Grandmother

Just before her death the following selected Scriptures were sent to her grandmother and hand delivered.

"Behold! I tell you a mystery. We shall not all sleep, but we shall all be changed, in a moment, in the twinkling of an eye, at the last trumpet. For the trumpet I have fought the good fight, I have finished the race, I have kept the faith. Henceforth there is laid up for me the crown of righteousness, which the Lord, the righteous judge, will award to me on that Day, and not only to me but also to all who have loved his appearing." (2 Timothy 4:7-8)

"For I am sure that neither death nor life, nor angels nor rulers, nor things present nor things to come, nor powers, nor height nor depth, nor anything else in all creation, will be able to separate us from the love of God in Christ Jesus our Lord." (Romans 8:38-39)

"The trumpet will sound, and the dead will be raised imperishable, and we shall be changed. For this perishable body must put on the imperishable, and this mortal body must put on immortality. When the perishable puts on the imperishable, and the mortal puts on immortality, then shall come to pass the saying that is written: "Death is swallowed up in victory." "O death, where is your victory? O death, where is your sting?" (John 11:25-26)

Jesus said to her, "I am the Resurrection and the Life. Whoever believes in me, though he die, yet shall he live, and everyone who lives and believes in me shall never die. Do you believe this?" (1Corinthians 2:9) (There was always an affirmative "yes" to this question, when it was presented to the grandmother.)

What no eye has seen, nor ear heard, nor the heart of man imagined, what God has prepared for those who love him. (Revelation 14:13)

And I heard a voice from heaven saying, "Write this: Blessed are the dead who die in the Lord from now on." "Blessed indeed," says the Spirit, "that they may rest from their labors, for their deeds follow them!" (Romans 14:7-9)

"For none of us lives to himself, and none of us dies to himself. For if we live, we live to the Lord, and if we die, we die to the Lord. So then, whether we live or whether we die, we are the Lord's. For to this end Christ died and lived again, that he might be Lord both of the dead and of the living." (<u>Philippians 1:21-23</u>)

"For to me to live is Christ, and to die is gain. If I am to live in the flesh, that means fruitful labor for me. Yet which I shall choose I cannot tell. I am hard pressed between the two. My desire is to depart and be with Christ, for that is far better." (<u>Revelation 21:4</u>)

"He will wipe away every tear from their eyes, and death shall be no more, neither shall there be mourning, nor crying, nor pain anymore, for the former things have passed away." (<u>James 1:12</u>)

"Blessed is the man who remains steadfast under trial, for when he has stood the test he will receive the crown of life, which God has promised to those who love him." (Psalm 1:1)

"So is it with the resurrection of the dead. What is sown is perishable; what is raised is imperishable. It is sown in dishonor; it is raised in glory. It is sown in weakness; it is raised in power. It is sown a natural body; it is raised a spiritual body. If there is a natural body, there is also a spiritual body." (<u>1 Corinthians 15:42-44</u>)

"You have been born again, not of perishable seed but of imperishable, through the living and abiding word of God; for all flesh is like grass and all its glory like the flower of grass. The grass withers, and the flower falls, but the word of the Lord remains forever." (<u>1 Peter 1:23-25</u>)

And he said, "Naked I came from my mother's womb, and naked shall I return. The LORD gave, and the LORD has taken away; blessed be the name of the LORD." (<u>Job 1:21</u>)

Part 4

Thomas A Kempis, Meditation on Death

The Imitation of Christ
Translated by Fr. Leo Sherley- Price, Penguin Books, 1952
Book One Chapter 23, page 57

"Very soon the end of your life will be at hand; consider, therefore, the state of your soul. Today a man is here; tomorrow he is gone." (I Macc. ii, 63) "And when he is out of sight, he is soon out of mind. Oh, how dull and hard is the heart of man, which thinks only of the present, and does not provide against the future! You should order your every deed and thought, as though today were the day of your death. Had you a good conscience, death would hold no terrors for you." (Luke xii, 37) even so, it were better to avoid sin than to escape death. (Wis. iv, 16) "If you are not ready to die today, will tomorrow find you better prepared?"(Matt.xxiv, 44)"Tomorrow is uncertain; and how can you be sure of tomorrow? Of what use is a long life, if we amend so little? Alas, a long life often adds to our sins rather than to our virtue."

*This brief meditation about this book was written by a member of the Congregation of the Common Life, founded by Gerard Groote. The author was born in 1380 in Kempen in what today is Belgium. The original text was in Flemish and was first circulated in Holland. The work has been translated into many languages and is also widely known as one of the most published books since the Gutenberg Bible first appeared in Germany. There is little doubt that this text has been preached from many pulpits over the past four centuries.

Other Testimonies about Death and Near Death

The Near Death of Joe

Accidental death is always very sad and troubling for everyone who is close to the person dying. Joe's near death might have been at the scene of the accident or in an ambulance on the way to a hospital ER.

In his little sedan Joe was calmly crossing a busy intersection on a green light when a transport truck went through a red light and struck Joe's car on the driver's side rear door. The truck was going fast enough to spin the car around several times, leaving it abandoned in the intersection. The car behind his vehicle pushed the still standing car off to the side.

This entire scene was observed by an ambulance crew at a fast-food restaurant across the street. They rushed out the door and put Joe's motionless body into a pressure bag. They were not sure at the time but suspected broken ribs and possible punctured lung. If not treated almost immediately, this injury would surely have caused his death.

Their suspicion was correct, and the solution did save his life. He got to the hospital where the punctured lung was repaired. After a few days of recuperating, he was discharged and went home.

Joe continues to attend Mass as often as possible and is very thankful that his life was extended for more than the fateful day when he almost became a traffic statistic.

Nick's Sad Lifetime of Near Death

Erin and I were walking in a mall on a rainy day when a lady working in a bakery restaurant noticed my attention to the menu on the wall. She also noticed that I had some difficulty reading the sign, so she handed me the printed version. She commented on the Benedictine crucifix I was wearing, which provided an opportunity for telling her that she was talking to a "dead man." That quickly led into her own, personal story of life and death.

This story comes from the fifty-eight-year-old daughter of a man, who spent a life of dissipation and lived with the effects of constant cigarette smoking, heavy drinking, and unhealthy eating habits for most of his adult life.

Gloria related that she and her mother would make several trips to the hospital each year, following an ambulance in which her dad was yet again a high-risk patient. This started when she was only five years old.

This yearly pattern became so common to them that she could not remember a time when her father was not gasping for breath or in some form of severe pain. The sad irony of his life was that he continued to smoke and drink heavily, paying no attention to his diet nor making any attempts to exercise. Nick was a respiratory and cardiovascular lifetime disaster. In addition to all his physical problems, he was constantly angry at just about everything and everyone.

Gloria and her mother would pray and go to church, hopeful that prayers might help with this slow-motion family tragedy. The problem was only made worse by the frequent trips to the ER and subsequent attempts to get him to make some effort to improve his destructive lifestyle.

Later when Gloria had a family of her own, she continued to grieve about her mother and father. The tragedy in her life was so great that Gloria had given up on God. With no change for too many years there was little, or no hope left. The final stage of her despair was interrupted with a call from a hospital on the day immediately before her father's death.

In a voice that could only be described as a whisper, Nick was able to apologize to Gloria, and ask for her forgiveness for all the pain and suffering he had caused in her life. She could barely speak a consoling word through all her tears. She did, however, come to some resolution that her dad had finally come to grips with his lifetime of anger and blaming God for all his problems.

Gloria made it to the hospital ER waiting room, coinciding with the time that her dad's body was being moved to the morgue. Greeted with many tears and hugs from family, she was beginning to be consoled for the lifetime of regret and resentment surrounding her dad's lifetime of near death.

She also described an experience her father had recounted of his insight into life after death: that there is another dimension to life when one dies. He shared that during one of the ambulance trips to the hospital, he was separated from his body and floated above the ambulance where he could see himself in his unresponsive, physical body. It was frantically being worked on by paramedics, and he noted that "they were doing it all wrong." Two days later he woke up, discovering that he had returned to his body in a hospital bed.

As Erin and I said good-bye, we were both in tears of joy for Gloria. We continue to marvel at the power of love and the healing strength of forgiveness in relationships between fathers and daughters.

Death at 82 and Still Living

This account was shared with me at the airport. We were waiting for a flight from Denver to Toronto after the Baptism of our 23rd grandchild in late August 2019. The man sitting next to me was talking on his phone to business partners and the content was easily overheard. He would be back in Ontario in time for the next big sales meeting with the European customers for their product line. After his call ended, I asked him about the type of farm equipment he was selling and installing on site. He was keen to explain his all new and very successful cattle moveable cage raising program that brought him to Colorado.

He commented about my Benedictine crucifix, which provided an opportunity to use my now well practiced line of evangelism. He seemed open to tell me of his families' faith background. That led to my usually unexpected statement about the person on my end of the conversation: "You are looking at and listening to a dead man." After asking what that meant and hearing my abbreviated story, he seemed quite eager to share his version of end of life in his own family.

When his mother was 82, she was rushed to a hospital with the classic presentation of a heart attack. Their parish priest was the first person called. The pastor arrived to pray with her, but she was already dead, and it was too late to hear her last Confession and receive the Last Rites of the Church.

Shortly after the priest left her room, the duty nurse discovered a pulse and additional medical support was rushed to her by the cardiac staff. After a period of stabilization, she was able to have cardiac bypass surgery with complete success.

Her son was happy to report that "she is doing very fine now," fifteen years later. She goes bowling and has many hobbies. He added with a smile and a bit of irony, that after hearing about her car breaking down, he had directed her to the keys for his new Ford Mustang convertible.

His latest project had now become the need for a new car. "Mom has stolen my new Mustang. The first thing I must do when I get home is to buy another car!"

The Death and Survival x 3 of Hans

After sharing my story and talking about the recently published book, Hans just listened carefully but said nothing in response to my incredible story. Then without hesitation he said, "Good for you, but you know I died and came to life again on three separate occasions." That statement sure got my attention, while visiting at the coffee and doughnuts social after Mass.

Hans started his personal witness of how faith in Jesus Christ as his Savior and Lord was the central focus of his life. He then moved on with the story of his first trip to an ER. He had died. The medical staff in the ER transported him immediately to Neurosurgery for what sounds like a scene from a modern horror movie. The top of his scalp and skull were removed to release the tremendous pressure of the rare double stroke, which had caused his death. After a period of resuscitation and stabilization his skull was replaced and scalp was sewed back in place. There was no question that he was telling the truth as the visible evidence of the procedure was quite apparent from the almost hidden scar on his forehead. Human beings often die from a stroke affecting one side or the other, but this survival was truly remarkable. There was only the slightest indication of residual damage, as his speech--like my own--was slightly hesitant at certain points in his story.

His second story was less dramatic but equally incredible. His body was dragged lifeless from the bottom of a swimming pool. A quick check for a pulse and respiration provided no evidence of life. The lifeguard on duty went ahead with artificial respiration as best he could. After prolonged efforts without response the lifeguard had almost given up, when a large amount of water was forcibly discharged, and Hans began to breathe on his own again.

The third and perhaps most spectacular survival was an extremely painful episode with evidence that remained clearly visible. Severe burn victims have telltale damaged skin: the surface is mottled and looks like the outside of a prune. The top of his shirt was slightly opened to expose the evidence of the extremely painful burns that covered the greater part of his body.

Hans had worked for years doing flooring of all kinds. On the fatal day of his last job he was trying to remove some very stubborn carpet from a cement floor. The flammable solvent he was using to peel up the rug reached a space heater nearby, which caught fire and engulfed the room in flames. He was pronounced dead by suffocation at the scene of the accident, but an observant ER staff member detected minute signs of life. Hans spent an entire year and a half in rehabilitation. The initial painful survival took weeks of careful treatment. Months went into extended periods of skin graft surgery with limited undamaged areas to replace the painful and scorched skin. I was practically in tears by the time he reached the end of his story and I could see that it was not easy to move through the memory of the trauma. He ended on the note that God had spared his life these three times and he could only thank Him with the rest of his life and prayer.

The Death and Survival of Betty

While chatting about winter stays in Florida over many years to the lady next to me on a flight, I was able to slip in my typical opener about my death at age fifty, when the topic moved to retirement and old age. After listening carefully to my testimony, she looked over to me and with tears in her eyes told me about the death of her dear mother in Florida.

She had boarded an ambulance with her eighty-year-old mom. All the medical indicators were standard for a massive heart attack and impending threat to her life. The ambulance crew did all the typical protocol in transit, and by the time Betty was rushed into ER, it was clear that the end was near. However, the lady telling me this incredible story was a self-professed Catholic and from a family of prayer for several generations. With modern telecommunications the whole family was alerted to pray for mom, grandma, and great grandma. The waiting room scene included a few other family members from nearby.

There were no conversations expressing anxiety and "what if" reactions. The family members continued to pray the rosary. The fateful appearance of one of the ER doctors included the results of all of their efforts to save Betty's life with care and concern. The heart attack was fatal, and she died without pain and prolonged suffering.

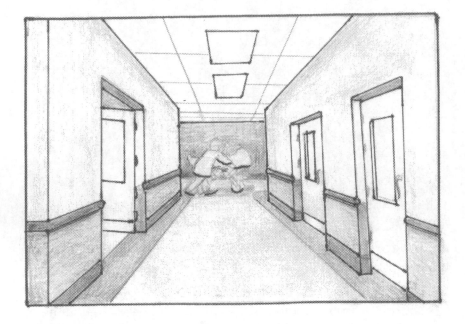

The family was surprisingly unshaken by this news and could only share the joy that mom had gone to be with the Lord. However, after a while the silence of the waiting room was shattered by a doctor from the morgue who came out shouting. "She is still alive. I can hardly believe it!"

There had not been time for a death certificate to be filed, but the time of death was recorded as 10:02 a.m. The family noted that the time on the waiting room clock when the doctor from the morgue had burst in with the news was 10:17 a.m. So, Betty had been clinically dead for fifteen minutes. Follow up examination of Betty's survival showed no impairment or lack of mental functions or abilities.

This flight was different from the many other returns to our summer place. I am happy to report this conversation as another incredible story of the impact of prayer and the mercy of God's intervention in what by all definitions is impossible.

The Biblical description of the life and death of Lazarus relates to Betty's story of the power of prayer twenty centuries later. No medical intervention could be used to explain what had happened, but she is still alive. The episode from the New Testament that best applies to Betty's survival appears in Acts 20:7-10.

On the first day of the week (Sunday, in Troas) when we were gathered together to break bread, Paul talked with them intending to depart on the morrow, and he prolonged his speech until midnight.

There were many lights in the upper chamber where we were gathered. And a young man named Eutychus was sitting in the window. He sank into a deep sleep as Paul talked still longer; and being overcome by sleep, he fell down from the third story and was taken up dead. But Paul went down and bent over him, and embraced him said, "Do not be alarmed, for his life is in him."

Paul's immediate response was that faith in Jesus would provide for Eutychus to come alive after he was claimed to be dead. And in like manner it can be said that Betty's daughters and others, who were praying in faith, had the same result for her.

Years of Christian ministry comedy material have developed on the Eutychus text. Any priest or pastor who is told his homily was very much like the one that Paul gave in Acts 20, or that the congregation was paying attention just like Eutychus would be forced to review the meaning of possible consequences.

Betty had been pronounced dead, and the typical concern is the amount of brain damage after an extended period of no respirations. The next question was a real leap of faith. I timidly asked how her mom came out of this trauma.

I was prepared for the worst concerning the question about Betty's status and the frequently serious debilitation of life in a wheelchair or a permanent paralysis common to stroke victims. To my great relief and joy, she asked if I wanted to meet her mom? and said, "She's right next to me." All this time Betty had been listening from the next seat. She gave me a coy smile and clearly demonstrated that, "I'm just fine for an 82-year-old woman who once was dead but now is alive as ever." So, I remain very blessed to have the privilege to recount this miraculous story of survival for all the readers of this book.

The Tragic Death and Survival of Michael

When a crime is the reason for a death it can only be called a tragedy. In the case of Michael's death, the crime was a brutal attack on a downtown street of large Canadian city. We first became aware of what had happened when his mother, a faithful member of our parish prayer group, called us from the hospital to ask if we could come to pray over Michael. He and his mother had been members of our small prayer group for several years. His insights and sharing were always a blessing to all of us. The news of his precarious condition was heavy on all of our hearts.

Our dear friends and leaders of the prayer group (Edwin and Anita) picked us up for the stressful car ride to the hospital hidden in the middle of skyscrapers. The location was complicated and the hospital was not the typical driveway up to a large building with "Hospital" and a large H on the roof. In this case, the real trouble was finding the front door. At street level with no obvious signs we only had our GPS to guide us to the small lobby with multiple elevator doors. We got to the sixth floor to meet Sophie for the very emotional and stressful encounter with her and then with her son Michael.

He was attending a post-secondary school not far from the hospital. He was innocently walking back to his little apartment when a group of four men walked up and began to attack him. He was left for dead after the use of multiple baseball bat strikes to his head. The tragic result was not only a crushed skull but a mutilated left hemisphere.

The terrible results of this senseless attack were similar to gunshot wound to the head on one side. The tissue damage can only be described as irreparable. The real tragedy of this crime was the police report that the one man, who was captured at the scene with the help of a passerby, confessed, "That guy we beat up is not the one we were after." It was a case of mistaken identity!

When we reached the sixth floor the scene was particularly frightening for me. All the reminders of the smells, sights, and noises of an ER ward were all too clear in my personal memory of the scene of my own death, as reported in Dead Man Watching. We were not in an ordinary ER but a brain trauma ward, specializing in stroke and head accident cases. The specialist had recently informed Sophie that she should be prepared for the worst, and that if Michael survived he would be in a vegetative state for the remainder of his life.

Upon entering his room the sight was frightening to the point of wanting to run away because of everything I saw, smelled and heard. If the ER sights and sounds of my own death were scary, then this particular brain trauma room was a horror film of flashing lights, wires and tubes inserted into a motionless body. The sight of Michael was almost more than I could handle. It took all the courage I had to join in the prayers over what seemed to be a corpse in a hospital gown. His face was distorted with eyes closed and a large cloth helmet with hoses and wires attached to blinking and beeping machines surrounding the bed. There was hardly room for the four of us around his bed. Anita took the lead in praying for God's mercy and the sparing of his life. As we continued to pray over Michael the only area to place my own hand onto his was his left hand. His hand was ice cold, and my heart fainted as I was sure he was dead.

At the conclusion of this mission of mercy there was no visible evidence that any change had taken place. We softly sang a few songs of praise and thanksgiving and left the room, as a nurse looked at us curiously, as though we were acting that a miracle would happen.

A short meeting with Sophie in the ward waiting room allowed us to pray with her in this hour of prolonged suffering. We wandered out of the maze of the hospital and drove back home with minimal conversation.

It would be the end of the week before Sophie could call with signs of hope, as his condition did not worsen but had shown some small indicators of improvement. In view of the specialist's warnings to expect death or life in a coma, this was good news.

Michael spent the next six weeks of intensive care with growing hope of return to some of his former abilities. It started with getting out of bed by himself and physiotherapy to use his right leg and hand again. With additional time and effort, Michael is doing very well for a man with only half a brain and the crippling results of this tragic crime that ends on a very positive note. Michael is making a remarkable recovery, as he is walking, talking and processing complex information. We all remain thankful for all that Jesus has done and continues to do in this precious life.

The Death and Survival of Loreto

Loreto was born and raised a Catholic in a small hamlet in Puglia, Italy, the area famous as the origin of the "best spaghetti in all of Italy" because of the quality of the durum wheat (*granadura* in Italian) grown there. His story was brought to us by Deacon Carlo in our Canadian parish when he found out about my new book.

At a very young age Loreto contracted scarlet fever and was found dead in his bed. He was given the Last Rites by the parish priest who was present at his death. The regional, itinerate doctor pronounced him dead and signed his death certificate at the provincial magistrate's office.

The total amount of time before his miraculous awakening was not known, but he had been dead for many hours and possibly as much as an entire day. The local population in the region quickly became aware of this extraordinary event and people began to arrive at his modest home. He and his family tried without success to avoid people as much as they could. When he began to speak words of caution to some individuals about hidden personal secrets and their errant way of life, he began to experience even more trouble than could have been expected. He was criticized in public and the parish priest had to make pronouncements at Mass about not judging what God had done in Loreto's life and why people might benefit from his prophetic messages.

There were a number of occasions throughout his troubled life in which he could not have known what he was talking about, because he was never there. On one occasion he brought a message from a man that had been dead for many years to his widow. It was about the funeral when her husband was buried in another man's shirt. It seems somewhat peculiar that this supernatural transmission should be made over an incorrect burial outfit, but it remains an event that was true and had great meaning to the widow, because she had grieved for all those years about her husband's final judgment and where he was. Her consolation from Loreto was that the dead man was in fact in heaven and she could finally be at peace.

Loreto did not live into old age but died naturally at fifty two. His life and two deaths remain a mystery, as challenging as the many times when people in the Bible were brought to life after they were clearly dead.

The Death and Survival of Jared

Jared was in a terrible auto accident and was pronounced dead in an ER of those injuries. His miraculous recovery would eventually leave him paralyzed for the remainder of his life. He testified to members of family that he saw Jesus when he went to heaven. He was told by medical staff that his life would move forward, but not as it had been. After a period in a coma he woke up to find that he had no sensations below his neck. With some rehabilitation help and a lot of help and prayer from his friends and family he was able to progress to the stage of competing in handicapped games. In fact, he managed to win medals three times in the Special Olympics.

It was surprising to find out that he is married and has four healthy children. I don't mean to sound disrespectful, and I'm guessing you are wondering also, but "how does that work when you are almost completely paralyzed?" He has become a motivational speaker and travels widely to give his testimony. There is also the amazing story of the man born with no arms or legs who is a father and motivational speaker, too. Both of these men have stories of how faith has brought them through it all.

When I found out about Jared from his uncle, he was reported to be almost forty years old and quite successful in his careers as a motivational speaker and a full time husband and dad.

Actually, I found out about Jared after introducing myself as the author of a book with that title and the fact that another book was being completed with stories like my own. While I did not get permission from Jared himself, his uncle said it would be an honor to hear that this witness would become a chapter in my next book.

The Near Death of Jenny

This story was brought to my attention at a pro-life support dinner held near our winter home. Our life saving ministry on a street in that city happens twice a week in front of a "women's health center" (i.e., abortion clinic).

A conversation with the guest to one side was providential to the writing of this book. After hearing about my death and the book that was composed years later, Barbara started to tell me about a miracle that took place in her marriage.

In 1967 their first child was born with unusual challenges. Jenny was physically handicapped. Her body was diminutive and deformed, indicating that she would grow up as a "dwarf" with some of the typical difficulties. This condition included enlarged joints with small arms and legs. It was not discovered by a doctor at the time of birth, but she was also born totally deaf. This challenging fact was observed by a carpenter. While working on Barbara's kitchen, he noticed that the newborn baby did not respond to his loud hammering on the cupboards. Sure enough, Jenny would live all her life without sound.

Her condition would become formidable to overcome, as well known from the Helen Keller. For Jenny the road ahead included good sight but difficulty in speaking because of a physical malformation of her pallet.

The real witness of Christian faith in this story was at the time of delivery. The doctor could have used any of dozens of considerate statements to alert Barbara to the condition of her new daughter.

He said, "This child is not worth keeping because she has so many problems." May God forgive that doctor for what has now become far too common in contemporary obstetrics around the world. As a result of modern imaging and pre-birth testing many doctors suggest abortion to avoid the difficulties of a "problem child."

Barbara reacted with love, kindness and a lot of prayer and faith for her new, little, struggling baby daughter. Regardless of the doctor's apparent condemnation of this newborn gift from God, Barbara and her supportive husband would raise their new daughter in a family of love and caring.

Her witness story concluded with Barbara's smile about the recent celebration of Jenny's fifty-second birthday in 2019.

I took a bold step to ask if she had gotten married, and the answer was a surprise as big as the story: "Yes, she is married and has two very healthy children." It is essential to say that faith in Jesus Christ was and is the central aspect of this heartwarming testimony.

The Near Death of Daniel

At fifty years old Daniel was a healthy, athletic man with a life full of energy and risk-taking adventures. This all nearly ended with a gust of wind.

He was soaring and gliding through the dazzling, panoramic skies of the American southwest desert. His hobby at that time is called backpack parachute gliding. The equipment includes a small gasoline engine, attached to a fan within a cage, which looks like a large old fashion, desk fan. The backpack weighs fifty pounds. The pilot runs along the ground until the large canopy of thin fabric fills with air and lifts off the ground.

The thrill of it all ended at fifty feet, when he was about to land, and the chute hit a down draft--common to the flight sequence. However, when this happens at a higher altitude, the chute refills with air again and works as expected. He was too low! Within seconds the aeronautic capacity to keep his two-hundred-and-forty-pound body and the apparatus in the air became a colorful flag plunging to the desert floor below. Even though he had been flying several thousand feet up, the descending conclusion did not leave room for the canopy to fill with the necessary air to provide for the typical soft, running landing.

Daniel hit the hard sand with both feet from a height that was estimated to be fifty feet. The surface was as hard as concrete, and the impact was shattering. Some observers called 911. An ambulance arrived twenty minutes later with paramedics gently loading him onto a stretcher. The lower half of his body was described as a "dangling pair of pants." His vital signs were good, but there was serious damage to his lower body. The excruciating pain was deadened by the body's natural protector as he went into shock followed by using morphine. The first ER doctor to see Daniel was amazed that he had even survived the impact.

The damage to his lower body was substantial: two broken legs in multiple places, a broken pelvis and both ankles shattered. No wonder the first orthopedic surgeon to see him said he could save him a lot of pain and suffering by amputating both of his legs just below his pelvic area. The reconstruction program was possible but long and painful with the subscript of an enormous cost. Without insurance it would surely be financial ruin for a lifetime. Daniel's immediate answer was to save both legs and endure all the unforeseen problems.

The intense surgeries took many hours to complete and each one was only the pathway to the next one...months later. The installation of multiple screws, plates and stainless-steel rods took hours of surgery with several months between each recovery. Complications set in with deep bone infections requiring antibiotics in heavy dosage, resulting in the typical GI disaster. All these problems complicated the recovery from each surgery.

The bill for all this specialist activity was astronomical. At the end of it all, his medical bill was one million and five hundred thousand dollars. What a blessing that it was totally covered by his insurance policy.

The answer to the many prayers for Daniel had been granted. He is now able to walk without crutches. His long recovery period had included a Christian counselor with prayer for healing.

After it all, he and several other prayer group partners took on a ministry of going to local penitentiaries to witness about the power of God in all their lives.

The team is made up of men who were either wounded military or accident victims with various incredible stories of recovery.

The typical question of many about why a life is spared from death remains a mystery. Lazarus seems at first to have disappeared after his miraculous survival, but many came to him to hear about his life, death and being raised by Jesus, which became the source of many conversions.

This story leads to the next one about the pastor who helped Daniel through the mental, emotional and spiritual trauma of his fall from the sky.

Pastor Mathew's Near Death

Pastor Mathew's prayer and inspiration for and with Daniel was pivotal to his recovery when discouragement was a major daily problem. The deep bone infections were long processes and very wearing.

Twenty years earlier Mathew was the youth pastor at the time of the momentous change in his life. A school bus from the small church, where Mathew served, was pulling out of the church parking lot for a picnic, when everyone inside felt a thump in the rear of the bus. Mathew was trying to help with the backup around a difficult corner, but the driver could not see him in any of the mirrors. Everyone in the bus rushed out the door at the screams of pain from under the bus. Two of the double wheels had crushed one arm, both legs and caused a neck injury. An ambulance was on scene within a reasonable time. The paramedics quickly injected Mathew with a pain killer and carefully placed him onto a stretcher.

The whole church community was alerted to pray for him, and all did. He spent several weeks in painful physical rehabilitation with surprising results. The amount of daily prayer for Mathew was a major part of his rapid recovery. He continues to witness to the mercy of God whenever possible. Just to see him walking around without any impairment is a visible sign to all who know his background story.

Denny's Lifetime of Close Calls and Death

The Denny in this story is the same good friend that was a major part of my story at the beginning of this book. He is the same faithful man along with his dear wife Margaret Ann, who introduced us to life saving on Tuesdays and Thursdays in Florida.

Denny was raised in a Catholic environment with no regressions or diversions. The first great challenge in his life was a diagnosis of inflammatory bowel disease at age eighteen that left him bed ridden for months. He saw life passing him by with the question of how long he would have to live with this painful and distracting condition. Discouragement was a major part of this period as anyone suffering with the condition. The medical and surgical conclusion took place at age twenty-six with a colostomy. This resection of the bowel meant that he would carry around a collection bag for the rest of his life. It was a mystery to me how he could go swimming in later life in Florida? I never quite made it to ask him this sensitive question.

He became a very successful salesman for a national brand of apparel. He married and had a family with more or less normal progress through the stages of family life. After all the time in a Catholic faith context, he had a Pauline experience at age fifty when he was inspired to quit his job and "go to work with the poor." His boss refused to accept his resignation multiple times, but was forced to hire a new man when it was clear that Denny would not be coming back.

Working with the poor was a dramatic change from their middle-class suburban life, as they traveled into Indianapolis to serve in a downtown soup kitchen operated by a Catholic organization. The clientele was predominantly requiring basic survival assistance. Daily challenges dealing with the homeless and generational poverty required perseverance, kindness, and prayer to navigate through the bad body odors, smell of alcohol, dirty faces, and drooling mouths. Then there were people in drug induced confusion.

Denny and Margaret Ann were completely out of their social element, but their selfless motivation was evident; thus, some of the people instinctively appreciated their authentic kindness and desire to help. Denny always wore a Benedictine crucifix and was approachable, and there were many requests to pray for those in need with ailments and sicknesses. A few returned each week, expressing thanks for answered prayers.

During this time the abortion disaster taking place, as a result of the pivotal Roe vs Wade Supreme Court decision to legalize the death of the innocent unborn babies, motivated the couple to become active members of sidewalk counseling. It must be emphasized that they were not protesters or picketers common to the period of protesting the war in Vietnam. Their activities were focused on offering helpful information and hope to women, asking them to reconsider their often uninformed, hasty and pressured decisions. They provided options for many practical supports, such as counseling, housing, diapers, etc. for those in need of assistance. Most of all they encouraged them to become mothers who would protect and care for their babies and, in some cases, choose adoption as a loving alternative.

All the time their ministry at the soup kitchen and lifesaving was in progress, Denny's own life was at risk due to another medical threat. This time it was multiple myeloma, a typically fatal form of cancer. He went through the only form of treatment available at the time with a lot of prayer from family, friends, and faith communities. Many years passed, when the same threat returned after an initial medical recovery from the first bout. This time he went to a Christian healing service where he was slain in the Spirit. There are many cases in the Bible of persons who were knocked off their feet and went through some dramatic conversion or change in their lives (e.g., Paul on the road to Damascus). Denny was prayed with and gently fell to the floor for an extended period of time, during which he felt what he described as being infused with intense heat throughout his entire body. The cure was complete, which was puzzling to his doctors and especially to his cancer specialist.

Denny went for many years free of any signs of a break in his remission. However, in early 2017 some pains and concerns brought him back to an oncologist. The prognosis was that the myeloma had returned. This time the drug therapies were much more diverse and able to target specific conditions. The treatments began during the last days of his winter stay in Florida and continued in his home town in Indiana. Through the summer of 2018 there were many prayers and a great deal of support from family and friends. Margaret Ann was at his side throughout the entire time of this end of life trial.

Denny went home to be with the Lord on Oct. 18, 2018. The funeral was held in Indiana, and the eulogy was delivered by his son-in-law. It is added here to illustrate this faithful life. The entire text is published here with the permission and gratitude of the family.

Eulogy for Denny

By Greg

Good Morning. My name is Greg. I am a son-in-law of Denny, and I am humbled by this opportunity to speak on behalf of the family to provide a celebratory summary of Denny.

It is difficult to summarize Denny in just a few words or a few minutes. I am confident that everyone sitting here that was lucky to know Denny could spend hours communicating how Denny affected, impacted or changed their lives. His passion and enthusiasm for life and God were contagious, and he had a way of being able to communicate to all of us.

There are many remarkable things that come to mind, when I think of Denny and the legacy he leaves here on earth:

*A devoted husband who loved Margaret Ann with all his heart. They were always together.

*A father that wanted to provide for his kids and share his love, wisdom, and knowledge on how to be a decent human being and see the good in all.

*A brother that cared for and loved his siblings no matter the ups and downs that a family faces.

*A friend who always had time for you and would help you if you needed anything. And finally....

*His Faith. Without question, Denny wanted to be the best disciple for Jesus Christ that he could be. He loved being a soldier for Jesus Christ.

Denny's faith more than anything is what set him apart. (His commitment, his focus and his passion for his faith).

I distinctly remember the first time I realized that Denny wasn't just quietly going about being a disciple of Christ. I was attending Mass with his daughter before we were married and was sitting next to Denny. When the first song started, I nearly jumped out of my skin when Denny started to belt out the notes. He was so energized and loud. Even all the little kids around Denny would turn and look at Denny with big eyes. No matter, because Denny was in his element and was so enthusiastically participating...just so happy to be in the presence of God.

Like everything, Denny was ALL IN.

Like his business career, ALL IN.

Like his gardening, ALL IN.

Like his healthy diets, ALL IN.

Like his family vacations, ALL IN.

With his faith he was ALL IN. Over time his devotion grew, and he worked hard to be what God wanted him to be. He evangelized to anyone who would listen. He wore a baseball hat that said Jesus is my Boss. His cars had bumper stickers plastered with faith. He wore a large cross around his neck. He wanted everyone to know that he worked for God.

He became a very prayerful man and always had a long list of people he prayed for. I know that list grew and names were changed, but I believe he was praying for 100 or so people.

His commitment for Pro-life that both Denny and Margaret Ann had was remarkable. He loved praying for those struggling women and helping them. It was wonderful to see them both glow when they had an assist in helping a mother change her decision.

He loved Mary and loved praying the rosary. His enthusiasm for this was genuine and pure. Even the last few days when he was not very coherent or could no longer speak, he still could pray the rosary. I witnessed first-hand Denny moving his lips, as we did a rosary with the family. God was present preparing Denny, as Denny was ministering to all of us with devotion to Mary. It was awesome.

Finally, I would like to say that this day is a celebration for Denny. It is hard for all of us to lose a man who was our husband, our father, our brother, and our friend. But Denny wanted nothing more than to be with Jesus. He truly, truly wanted nothing more than to be with Him.

He devoted his life to be a remarkable disciple of God and worked hard, so that he could rise and sit on the lap of Jesus. He set an example that all of us should strive for.

He is looking down on all of us, his hands are in the air, he is smiling ear to ear, shouting,

PRAISE YOU, JESUS! HALLELUJAH!

Thank you all for being here to celebrate Denny.

God Bless You All!

Pamela's Death under a City Bus

I talked with Pamela over lunch at a Catholic conference in Toronto in the spring of 2017. After briefly sharing about my story she also had a dramatic story of her survival from a traffic accident two years earlier.

She had just exited the rear door of a city bus she took daily to her job in downtown Toronto. She slipped on ice and fell to the curb. The driver made his standard right turn and had no idea that anything had happened until horns and lights caught his attention. Pamela had been run over and crushed between the rear tires and the curb. At first there was no sign of life, as she was in shock. Paramedics were on scene soon after the accident. Their first impression was that the victim was dead. Attempts to revive her seemingly lifeless body were successful, but the amount of injury was all too apparent, even to the curious crowd that quickly gathered. The ER room drama was intense, as her vital signs were erratic.

Once she had been successfully stabilized and moved to recovery, Pamela was barely coherent as relatives had been notified by looking up the ID information in her purse. She had conveniently included emergency contact names and her parish priest.

After weeks of rehabilitation at the same hospital, Pamela could not walk. She had two broken legs, six broken ribs, and a punctured lung. The healing process was accompanied by many prayers offered by friends and family, including her parish priest. When I met Pamela a few years later, after she had recovered from the trauma and was able to tell that her story had appeared in the local newspapers with the skeptical byline, "this is one to think about." How did Pamela manage to survive being run over by a bus? She and I knew the answer to that rhetorical question and can only praise God for His kindness and mercy.

Tommy's Near Death

We learned about Tommy's story from his widow. We met her after daily Mass at our home north of Toronto. A parked, small station wagon full of personal belongings, and the driver had yet to start her vehicle. The surprise was to find that her license plate was from Mississippi. Her window was open on the chilly morning, so I boldly asked if she was lost. Erin and I were surprised to find that she had spent the night in her car in the church parking lot in order to wait for Mass in the morning. So when we asked if she had already had breakfast, it gave us the opportunity to take her to our local favorite restaurant. The conversation over breakfast revealed that at she had been on the road for weeks all by herself. That night we insisted that she stay in our spare bedroom instead of her car. She had fascinating stories to tell and one was about her deceased husband. It was my blessing to receive the following chapter story to share with you.

Tommy was a field biologist working for the UN on a mission to help out with crop pests in Bolivia in the 1970's. His job was to consult with the land owners whose farms had pest problems. He had been assigned to the wealthy farmers but was also helping the poor and often destitute share croppers from the surrounding farms. On one fateful day Tommy was coaching one of the poor farmers when a well-dressed landowner in a black limo drove onto the scene. Instead of interrupting his conversation he asked the landowner to wait, while he completed his instructions with the poor farmer on how to deal with the pest problems on his small plot. When that was finished, he counseled the man in the limo.

Tommy went back to his hotel where he was told it was not safe to go out in public, because revolutionary soldiers were causing a lot of trouble in the city. He chose to ignore the warning and returned to his temporary UN office in a small courtyard near the local newspaper office. When he arrived he was faced by soldiers with machine guns and told to line up on the wall opposite of his UN office. After a brief prayer in desperation he had a sudden rush of peace and felt transported into the air in some way. It was amazing that he was calm and not panicked in view of the obvious threat that he and the other men in the lineup could be executed at any minute.

This scene of near death for Tommy was halted abruptly by the leader of the revolutionary gunmen in the firing squad lineup. He recognized Tommy from the previous day, as he was the limo driver for the landowner. He had observed that the landowner was made to wait while the poor farmer was instructed on how to save his little crop from destructive bugs.

The driver told the soldiers that Tommy was trying to help the common people of Bolivia and not just supporting the oppressive regime of the dictator and his military forces.

Needless to say, Tommy was very relieved that God had answered his prayers. He lived for many more years, as related by his dear wife.

The Near Death of Joe

Accidental death is always very sad and troubling for everyone who is close to the person dying. Joe's near death might have been at the scene of the accident or in an ambulance on the way to a hospital ER.

In his little sedan Joe was calmly crossing a busy intersection on a green light when a transport truck went through a red light and struck Joe's car on the driver's side rear door. The truck was going fast enough to spin the car around several times, leaving it abandoned in the intersection. The car behind his vehicle pushed the still standing car off to the side.

This entire scene was observed by an ambulance crew at a fast-food restaurant across the street. They rushed out the door and put Joe's motionless body into a pressure bag. They were not sure at the time but suspected broken ribs and possible punctured lung. If not treated almost immediately, this injury would surely have caused his death.

Their suspicion was correct, and the solution did save his life. He got to the hospital where the punctured lung was repaired. After a few days of recuperating, he was discharged and went home.

Joe continues to attend Mass as often as possible and is very thankful that his life was extended for more than the fateful day when he almost became a traffic statistic.

Nick's Sad Lifetime of Near Death before His Death

Erin and I were walking in a mall on a rainy day when a lady working in a bakery restaurant noticed my attention to the menu on the wall. She also noticed that I had some difficulty reading the sign, so she handed me the printed version. She commented on the Benedictine crucifix I always wear, which provided an opportunity for telling her that she was talking to a "dead man." That quickly led into her own, personal story of life and death.

This story comes from the fifty-eight year old daughter of a man, who spent a life of dissipation and lived with the effects of constant cigarette smoking, heavy drinking, and unhealthy eating habits for most of his adult life.

Gloria related that she and her mother would make several trips to the hospital each year, following an ambulance in which her dad was yet again a high risk patient. This started when she was only five years old.

This yearly pattern became so common to them that she could not remember a time when her father was not gasping for breath or in some form of severe pain. The sad irony of his life was that he continued to smoke and drink heavily, paying no attention to his diet nor making any attempts to exercise. Nick was a respiratory and cardiovascular life time disaster. In addition to all of his physical problems, he was constantly angry at just about everything.

Gloria and her mother would pray and go to church, hopeful that prayers might help with this slow-motion family tragedy. The problem was only made worse by the frequent trips to the ER and subsequent attempts to get him to make some effort to improve his destructive life style.

Later when Gloria had a family of her own, she continued to grieve about her mother and father. The tragedy in her life was so great that Gloria had given up on God. With no change for too many years there was little or no hope left. The final stage of her despair was interrupted with a call from a hospital on the day immediately before her father's death.

In a voice that could only be described as a whisper, Nick was able to apologize to Gloria, and ask for her forgiveness for all the pain and suffering he had caused in her life. She could barely speak a consoling word through all of her tears. She did, however, come to some resolution that her dad had finally come to grips with his lifetime of anger and blaming God for all of his problems.

Gloria made it to the hospital ER waiting room, coinciding with the time that her dad's body was being moved to the morgue. Greeted with many tears and hugs from family, she was beginning to be consoled for the lifetime of regret and resentment surrounding her dad's life time of near death.

She also described an experience her father had recounted of his insight into life after death: that there is another dimension to life when one dies. He shared that during one of the ambulance trips to the hospital, he was separated from his body and floated above the ambulance where he could see himself in his unresponsive, physical body. He was frantically being worked on by paramedics, and noted that "they were doing it all wrong." Two days later he woke up, discovering that he had returned to his body in a hospital bed.

As Erin and I said good-bye, we were both in tears of joy for Gloria. We continue to marvel at the power of love and the healing strength of forgiveness in relationships between fathers and daughters.

Death at 82 and Still Living and Laughing

This account was shared with me at the airport. We were waiting for a flight after the Baptism of our 23rd grandchild in late August 2019. The man sitting next to me was talking on his phone to business partners and the content was easily overheard. He would be back in Ontario in time for the next big sales meeting with the European customers for their product line. After his call ended, I asked him about the type of farm equipment he was selling and installing on site. He was keen to explain his all new and very successful cattle raising program that brought him to Colorado.

He commented about my Benedictine crucifix, which provided an opportunity to use my now well practiced line of evangelism. He seemed open to tell me of his families' faith background. That led to my usually unexpected statement about the person on my end of the conversation: "You are looking at and listening to a dead man." After asking what that meant and hearing my abbreviated story, he seemed quite eager to share his version of end of life in his own family.

When his mother was 82, she was rushed to a hospital with the classic presentation of a heart attack. Their parish priest was the first person called. The pastor arrived to pray with her but she was already dead, and it was too late to hear her last Confession and receive the Last Rite of the Church.

Shortly after the priest left her room, the duty nurse discovered a pulse and additional medical support was rushed to her by the cardiac staff. After a period of stabilization, she was able to have cardiac bypass surgery with complete success.

Her son was happy to report that "she is doing very fine now," fifteen years later. She goes bowling and has many hobbies. He added with a smile and a bit of irony, that after hearing about her car breaking down, he had directed her to the keys for his new Ford Mustang convertible.

His latest project had now become the need for a new car. "Mom has stolen my new Mustang. The first thing I have to do when I get home is to buy another car!"

Kelly's Near Death on a Horse Cart

Perhaps the most grievous loss of life is when a newborn dies. This tragic story starts with a premature gestation at only seven months with a delivery weight of only two pounds. Kelly had underdeveloped internal organs and lungs that were not prepared for breathing. She was taken out of the delivery room to a trauma unit on another floor.

Her mother was expecting to see her new baby but was told to wait while she was being cleaned up. After what seemed like an eternity she knew something was wrong. A priest had been called and Kelly was given the Last Rites of the Catholic Church even though her mother was Anglican.

With a great deal of medical intervention, Kelly was brought back to life despite the fact that several times during her first hours of life she had to be resuscitated. She was able to leave the hospital after a few weeks of care and monitoring to begin a normal life as a slightly smaller, energetic girl.

The second miraculous event in her life happened when 18 year old Kelly was out riding on her trotting cart in a rural area of Ontario. The horse was spooked by an animal in the thick grass and bolted toward a lake. They collided with a large log on the ground. The horse eventually broke away from the remaining parts of the cart leaving Kelly's badly injured body on the ground with a piece of the metal carriage punctured through her leg. Her first thought was of her mother, and how she would not be able to deal with her only daughter's death.

The ability to see from beyond her body was confirmed by being able to observe her mother driving down the road to find help. This would have been impossible from where her battered body lay in the low ditch where the accident happened. Furthermore, she also saw a group of gossamer, human-like figures watching over her and heard a voice say, "You will have pain beyond crying."

Another morning rider had seen the accident and called for medical help. When an ambulance did arrive, Kelly's vital signs were negligible. The paramedics heard the same words coming out of her in a faint voice: "You will have pain beyond crying." During the surreal scene going on before her eyes, she could see herself from above with all the events as clear as if she were actually overhead.

The ER doctors were alarmed at the amount of damage caused by the accident. Part of the metal cart had gone through her leg, and the major damage was the impact with the log, which broke several ribs and punctured several internal organs.

Their conclusion was that they would patch her up and hope for the best. All the time Kelly continued to plead with the consoling figures before her, telling them that she was not ready to leave her life and her dear mother all alone.

After an extended period of recovery, Kelly went on to get married, have a family and continue her life of faith. Her touching witness to me on a chance meeting in response to a car we had for sale in our driveway, led to a series of conversations in which she shared her story of death on a horse cart.

It all started after I showed her the classic car sign, I had just improved. When she arrived at the end, she was silent for several moments, but then blurted out that she had died too. Following that, she stopped talking.

My next response was to say that her story would be a blessing to include in this book, if she were willing. She did give permission and was given assurance that her real name would not be used to protect her privacy.

As was my experience and has been told by others before, she shared that for many years the emotions involved in her story were so upsetting that she had given up recounting the details to other people. The final straw was a close friend who cut short their friendship after she had shared about this miraculous intervention in her life. Her friend's initial response was the clue to her rejection, "that's too spooky for me."

Even as Kelly was telling her story, I could tell she was enthusiastic, but she was also dealing simultaneously with emotions linked to fear. The fear of death remains the ultimate human condition, but Kelly overcame that fear with faith. What else can be said as a reason for the incredible circumstances of her life and death?

Close-up of the Author's Benedictine Crucifix

Visions of What is Beyond as reported by Saint Faustina.

Diary of Saint Maria Faustina Kowalski (1905-1938) note 9, 27,1936 YouTube, history of Saint Faustina

Heaven: Today I was in heaven in spirit, and I see it's conceivable beauties and happiness now I understand Saint Paul who said, "Eye has not seen, nor ear has heard nor has it entered into the heart of man what God has prepared for those who love him."

Hell: Today I was led by an Angel to the chasm of hell. It is a place of great torture. The kind of torture I saw: the first torture that constitutes hell is the loss of God; the second is the perpetual remorse of conscience: the third is that one's condition will never change; the fourth is the fire that will penetrate the soul without destroying it, a terrible suffering, since it is purely spiritual fire lit by God's anger. The fifth torture is continual darkness and terrible suffocating smell, and despite the darkness the devils and the souls of the damned see each other and all the evil, both of hers and their own. The sixth torture is the constant company of Satan; the seventh torture is horrible despair, hatred of God, vile words, curses and blasphemy. There are special tortures destined for particular souls. I am writing this at the command of God, so that no soul may find excuse by saying there is no hell, or that nobody has or ever been there and so no one can say what Is like.

Purgatory: I was in a misty place full of fire in which there was a great crowd of suffering souls. They were praying fervently but to no avail for themselves, only we can come to their aid. I heard an interior voice which said my mercy does not want this, but my justice demands.

After all that has been said of life and death with faith in Jesus Christ, the best conclusion is:

No matter what happens, Immanuel God is with us.

"Create in me a clean heart, O God,
and put a new and right spirit within me" (Psalm 51:10).

"Let the words of my mouth,
and the meditation of my heart be acceptable in Thy sight,
O Lord, my rock and my Redeemer" (Psalm 19:14)

This entire story is about the mercy of God from beginning to multiple ends; it is a modern testimony of how God works in mysterious ways through and over many stages of life. The amazing revelation for all those who read these stories is that these are real people who died or almost died, and they are now talking to you about the miraculous interventions of God in death and life again. In a very real way this book is a collection of **auto-obituaries** of those who experienced their own deaths or near deaths and now live to tell their stories.

Dr, J. Roland Giardetti is a lifetime academic and published author in the fields of Fine Art, Art History, Photography, Secondary Education, Media, and Communications. This is his third work about Christian faith and dramatic testimonies of survival through lives of faith in Jesus Christ, as Lord and Savior.

THE final end.........and beyond?

Printed in the United States
by Baker & Taylor Publisher Services